Zimmermann/Freiburg-Braun

Aggression under the Rome Statute

Aggression under the Rome Statute

An Introduction

by

Andreas Zimmermann
Elisa Freiburg-Braun

2019

Published by
Verlag C. H. Beck oHG, Wilhelmstraße 9, 80801 München, Germany,
eMail: bestellung@beck.de

Co-published by
Hart Publishing, Kemp House, Chawley Park, Cumnor Hill, Oxford, OX2 9PH, United Kingdom,
online at: www.hartpub.co.uk

and

Nomos Verlagsgesellschaft mbH & Co. KG Waldseestraße 3–5, 76530 Baden-Baden, Germany,
eMail: nomos@nomos.de

Published in North America (US and Canada) by Hart Publishing,
c/o Independent Publishers Group, 814 North Franklin Street, Chicago, IL 60610, USA

Recommended citation:
Zimmermann/Freiburg-Braun, Aggression under the Rome Statute, mn. [#]

ISBN 978 3 406 70826 8 (C.H.BECK)
ISBN 978-1-5099-2405-9 (HART)
ISBN 978-3-8487-4678-1 (NOMOS)

© 2019 Verlag C.H.Beck oHG
Wilhelmstr. 9, 80801 München
Printed in Germany by
Kösel GmbH & Co. KG
Am Buchweg 1, 87452 Altusried-Krugzell
Typeset by
Reemers Publishing Services GmbH, Krefeld
Cover: Druckerei C.H.Beck Nördlingen

Table of Contents

Acronyms

I.
INTRODUCTION

1. Background

Under traditional rules of international law, no prohibition on the *jus ad bellum* did **1**
exist,[1] let alone a prohibition triggering the individual criminal responsibility for such
acts.[2] Rather, States engaged in warfare almost as a matter of routine. War therefore
constituted a reality of international relations, and remained an option at the disposal of
sovereign States in the exercise of their international relations. At most, while the resort
to war was traditionally considered legal as such, the only limits related to the emerging
norms of the *jus in bello*.[3] Yet, not the least due to the devastating experiences of World
War I and II in particular, States began to recognize that while war was a reality, it had
to be regulated. It followed that the international community increasingly recognized
the necessity to regulate not only the *jus in bello*, but maybe even more important the
jus ad bellum. At the same time, the idea of providing for individual criminal
responsibility for violations of the *jus ad bellum* also started to gain ground, be it only
slowly.

More specifically, and as is well-known, the devastations of World War I brought **2**
about the creation of the League of Nations. It was created, amongst other reasons, to
prevent (but not yet to prohibit as such) the resort to war. As a matter of fact, *inter
alia* Article 12 of the Covenant of the League[4] merely provided that the Members of
the League agreed that, if there should arise between them any dispute likely to lead
to a rupture, they will submit the matter either to arbitration or judicial settlement or
to enquiry by the Council of the League of Nations. They further agreed in no case to
resort to war *until three months after the award* by the arbitrators or the judicial
decision, or the report by the Council of the League on the matter, and hence only
provided for a cooling-off period, rather than outlawing resort to war as such.

It was then only the 1928 "General Treaty for Renunciation of War as an **3**
Instrument of National Policy", generally referred to as "Kellogg–Briand Pact" (or
Pact of Paris), in which its contracting parties undertook not to use war to resolve
"disputes or conflicts of whatever nature or of whatever origin they may be, which
may arise among them".[5]

The even larger-scale devastations caused by World War II, combined with the **4**
obvious inability of the League of Nations to prevent the outbreak of the war, led to
the demise of the League of Nations and the ensuing creation of the United Nations.

---

[1] See as to the historical development of the prohibition of the use of force: Dörr, "Use of Force,
Prohibition of", in: *MPEPIL*, mns. 4 *et seq.*; Kreß in: Barriga and Kreß (eds.), *The Crime of Aggression: A
Commentary*, 2017, 1; Hathaway/Shapiro, *The Internationalists: How a Radical Plan to Outlaw War
Remade the World*, 2017.

[2] See generally as to the historical development of the concept of individual criminal responsibility for
acts of aggression Sayapin, *The Crime of Aggression in International Criminal Law*, 2014, 147.

[3] See as to the historical development of the *jus in bello* Schwarz, "War Crimes", in: *MPEPIL*, mns. 3 *et
seq.*

[4] The Covenant of the League of Nations, https://treaties.un.org/doc/source/covenant.pdf (last accessed
May 2019).

[5] See generally on the content of the Briand-Kellogg-Treaty Lesaffer, "Kellogg-Briand Pact (1928)", in:
MPEPIL.

The latter was created to succeed the League of Nations in order to continue, among other reasons, its goal to prevent war, and, as the preamble of the Charter of the United Nations puts it eloquently, to thus "save succeeding generations from the scourge of war, which twice in our lifetime has brought untold sorrow to mankind".[6] As a result of these tragic, global experiences and the growing number of States borne from the remnants of war, the collapse of the mainly French and British colonial empire and colonialism, came the progressive development and further codification of international law,[7] including attempts by the General Assembly of the United Nations to codify applicable norms of the *jus ad bellum*.

5   In parallel, international human rights law was developing to strengthen the position of individuals *vis-à-vis* States.[8] Yet, the emerging system of human rights law did perceive individuals as the bearer of subjective *rights* only, but did not encompass the idea of individuals being individually *responsible* in case of violations of international law. In parallel, international humanitarian law, which, as mentioned, took the existence of armed conflicts somewhat as a fact of life, was developing further to regulate the means and methods of warfare, and to also provide greater protections for those not engaged in armed conflict.[9] With the adoption of the four Geneva Conventions in 1949, and the realization of the underlying normative concept of grave breaches thereof, the idea of individuals being individually responsible at least for violations of the *jus in bello* gained new ground. Yet, no parallel development took place as far as the *jus ad bellum* was concerned.

6   While over the years international law continued to develop into a wide array of areas including, but not limited to, topics such as the law of the sea,[10] the protection of the environment,[11] outer-space,[12] and the law governing the legal status of refugees,[13] the most relevant development when it comes to the topic at hand related to the maintenance of international peace and security, governed in particular by the Charter of the United Nations adopted in 1945. At the very heart of the UN Charter, rules were created and further strengthened regulating the use of force (*i.e.* the *jus ad bellum*) under international law. Generally speaking, under the Charter of the United Nations States may, first and foremost, use military force against other States, as well as against non-State armed groups,[14] when acting collectively within the framework of a mandate provided by the Security Council acting under Chapter VII,[15] or by virtue of a mandate provided by the General Assembly, acting under the *Uniting for*

---

[6] Wolfrum, in: Simma *et al.* (eds.), *The Charter of the United Nations. A Commentary*, 3[rd]ed., 2012, Preamble mn. 5; Hobe (ed.), *Die Präambel der UN-Charta im Lichte der aktuellen Völkerrechtsentwicklung*, 1997, 161.

[7] See generally on the process of the codification of international law Anderson *et al.* (eds), *The International Law Commission and the Future of International Law*, 1998; Llewellyn, "United Nations, Sixth Committee", in: *MPEPIL*, mns. 9 *et seq.*

[8] See generally on that development: Tomuschat, Human Rights – Between Idealism and Realism, 3nd ed., 2014, 1*et seq.*

[9] See as to the specific role of the Red Cross in the development of international law Geiß, Zimmerman and Haumer (eds.), *Humanizing the Laws of War: The Red Cross and the Development of International Humanitarian Law,* 2017.

[10] Rothwell and Stephens (eds.) *The International Law of the Sea*, 2010.

[11] Beyerlin and Marauhn (eds.), *International Environmental Law*, 2011.

[12] Von der Dunk and Tronchetti (eds.), *Handbook of Space Law*, 2015.

[13] See *inter alia* Zimmermann (ed.), *The 1951 Convention Relation to the Status of Refugees and its 1967 Protocol*, 2011.

[14] As to the issue of self-defence against armed attacks emanating from non-State actors see *inter alia* Peters and Marxsen, *ZaöRV* 2017, 3; Tams, *ZaöRV* 2017, 61.

[15] See Krisch, in: Simma *et al.* (eds.), *The Charter of the United Nations. A Commentary*, 3rd ed., 2012, Introduction to Chapter VII.

Peace Resolution,[16] or finally when States are acting in self-defence in accordance with Article 51 UN Charter.[17] Besides, there are somewhat more doubtful exceptions to the general prohibition of the use of force, their status under customary law being debatable, namely the concept of intervention upon invitation,[18] as well as the concept of humanitarian intervention.[19]

Alongside the creation of the United Nations, with the UN Charter embodying in its Article 2 (4) the concept of a general prohibition of the use of force *ad futurum*, the end of World War II also saw the establishment of two *ad hoc* military tribunals tasked to prosecute the major German and Japanese war criminals, *i. e.* the Nuremberg and Tokyo military tribunals.[20] These two tribunals had a mandate to, *inter alia*, and maybe even primarily, exercise jurisdiction over the "crime against peace" of aggression.[21] As a matter of fact, it was those tribunals that for the first time ever led to the punishment of individuals, by an international tribunal, for having committed the crime of aggression. **7**

Almost 30 years after the adoption of the UN Charter, it was in 1974 that the UN General Assembly drafted, and later adopted by consensus, Resolution 3314 (1974) on the definition of aggression.[22] What is most relevant for purposes of the issue of individual criminal responsibility for the crime of aggression is its Article 5 (2), which provides on the one hand that "[a]ggression gives rise to international responsibility", and on the other that "[a] war of aggression is a crime against international peace." The said resolution, in its Article 5, therefore somewhat already foreshadows the distinction, now contained in Article 8 *bis* of the Rome Statute, between aggression as such (now referred to as an act of aggression in the Rome Statute[23]) the ensuing consequences being a matter of the law of State responsibility on the one hand, and wars of aggression (now referred to as the crime of aggression in the Rome Statute[24]) on the other which might also entail individual criminal responsibility. **8**

What is more is that both, the International Court of Justice (ICJ), as well as the International Law Commission (ILC), have confirmed that, at least in contemporary international law, acts of aggression also constitute violations of a peremptory norm of international law (or *jus cogens*), and that a violation thereof also creates obligations owed to all States (or put otherwise that the said prohibition is of an *erga omnes* character).[25] **9**

---

[16] UN Doc A/RES/377 (3 November 1950); see also Klein and Schmahl in: Simma *et al.* (eds.), *The Charter of the United Nations. A Commentary*, 3rd ed., 2012, Art. 10, at 471.

[17] As to the requirements of Art. 51 UN Charter see Walter, in: Simma *et al.* (eds.), *The Charter of the United Nations. A Commentary*, 3rd ed., 2012, Art. 52; as well as *infra* mns. 182 *et seq.*

[18] See generally Nolte, *Eingreifen auf Einladung*, 1999; Nolte, "Intervention by Invitation", in: *MPEPIL*; Fox, "Intervention by Invitation', in: Weller (ed.) *The Oxford Handbook on the Use of Force in International Law*, 2015, 816. See also *infra* mns. 196 *et seq.*

[19] See generally Chesterman, *Just War or Just Peace?: Humanitarian Intervention and International Law*, 2002; Rodley, "Humanitarian Intervention', in: Weller (ed.) *The Oxford Handbook on the Use of Force in International Law*, 2015, 775. See also *infra* mns. 190 *et seq.*

[20] See Fuchs and Lattanzi, "International Military Tribunals', in: *MPEPIL*; Jescheck, "Nuremberg Trials', in: *EPIL* 1997, 747; Hosoya (ed.) *The Tokyo War Crimes Trial: An International Symposium*, 1986.

[21] See Article 6 a) Charter of the [Nuremberg] International Military Tribunal (8 August 1945), 82 UNTS 284; as well as Article 5 a) Charter of the International Military Tribunal for the Far East (19 January 1946), 4 BEVANS 20.

[22] As to the content of this resolution see, in particular, Bruha, "The General Assembly's Definition of the Act of Aggression', in: Barriga and Kreß (eds.), *The Crime of Aggression: A Commentary*, 2017, 142 (154); Bruha, *Die Definition der Aggression*, 1980.

[23] For details see *infra* mns. 104 *et seq.*

[24] For details see *infra* mns. 201 *et seq.*

[25] ICJ, *Case Concerning Barcelona Traction, Light and Power Co. Ltd* (*Belgium v. Spain*), Second Phase, *ICJ Reports* (1970), 3, para. 34; ICJ, *Military and Paramilitary Activities in and against Nicaragua*

10   Finally, and most importantly, as recently as 2010, and after decades of discussion, an amendment to the 1998 Rome Statute of the International Criminal Court (ICC) as to the inclusion of the crime of aggression was adopted at the Kampala conference. Also as a matter of treaty law,[26] it thus moved the issue of aggression beyond the rules of international law relating to State responsibility, but into the realm of individual criminal responsibility. As such, once the Court's jurisdiction over that crime is activated,[27] persons alleged to have committed the crime of aggression can be investigated and prosecuted by the ICC, assuming that the Court is able to exercise its jurisdiction over that individual *ratione loci* and *ratione personae*.

2. The crime of aggression in the Rome Statute: an overview

11   Ever since the negotiations on the possible creation of a permanent international criminal tribunal had started in 1994, it had become obvious that including the crime of aggression within the jurisdiction of the future ICC was never going to be an easy task, to say the least. When the Rome Statute of the ICC was finally adopted on 17 July 1998, the crime of aggression was left as a mere placeholder in what was then Article 5 (2) Rome Statute. It provided that the scope and definition of the crime, as well as the conditions under which the future ICC would eventually later exercise its jurisdiction, would have to be further discussed and eventually decided at a later date.[28] Put otherwise, while the negotiating States agreed that the crime of aggression was to be included within the Court's jurisdiction sometime in the future, they could not (or at least not yet) agree on how this could be eventually done.

12   From the very early stages of the negotiations on the creation of the ICC, States faced a number of significant challenges in their attempts to include the crime of aggression within the Court's jurisdiction, as they had been able to do with respect to the other three categories of core crimes, namely genocide, crimes against humanity and war crimes. While there had been attempts to also include additional crimes within the jurisdiction of the Court such as in particular terrorism and drug trafficking, it was only the three categories of genocide, crimes against humanity, as well as war crimes that found their way into the Rome Statute with the fourth, *i. e.* the crime of aggression, being in a state of limbo. As a matter of fact, trying to formulate a compromise between the competing interests and interpretations of States and their representatives seemed, as far as the crime of aggression was concerned, almost impossible. In particular, the two major challenges faced by States, when it came to the possible inclusion of the crime of aggression in the Rome Statute, were to provide for a definition of the crime in line with both, customary international law,[29] as well as the law of the Charter of the United Nations, and to define the possible role of the UN Security Council as far as the exercise of the Court's aggression-related jurisdiction was concerned.

(Nicaragua v. United States of America), Judgement (Merits), ICJ Rep. 1986, 14, 100, para. 190; International Law Commission, Commentary to Article 50 of its Draft Articles on the Law of Treaties, *ILC Yearbook* 1966, ii, 247.

[26] As to the concept of the crime of aggression under customary international law see Kreß in: Barriga and Kreß (eds.), *The Crime of Aggression: A Commentary*, 2017, 1 (7–9); Akande and Tzanakopoulos, in: Barriga and Kreß (eds.), *The Crime of Aggression: A Commentary*, 2017, 214 *et seq.*

[27] For details see *infra* mns. 16, 310 *et seq.*

[28] As to details for the content of Article 5 (2) Rome Statute, see *infra* mns. 83 *et seq.*

[29] As to the status of the crime of aggression under customary law see *inter alia* Kreß in: Barriga and Kreß (eds.), *The Crime of Aggression: A Commentary*, 2017, 1 (7–9); Akande and Tzanakopoulos, in: Barriga and Kreß (eds.), *The Crime of Aggression: A Commentary*, 2017, 214 *et seq.*

Obviously, the definition of the crime of aggression constituted the first main **13** challenge. As already briefly noted above,[30] the very notion of aggression came with a history with respect to its definition. In particular, a quite significant group of States supported the view that it was UN General Assembly Resolution 3314 (XXIX) that contained a sufficient definition which could be easily incorporated into the Rome Statute even for purposes of individual criminal responsibility. Other States did not feel that the said definition contained in UN General Assembly Resolution 3314 (XXIX) was reflective of customary international law at least as far as individual criminal responsibility was concerned. They therefore felt that there was a need to address some further questions surrounding the definition and the acts included within UN General Assembly Resolution 3314 (XXIX) before being able to agree upon a satisfactory language that would eventually fit the Rome Statute.

It ought to be noted, however, that although having the power to do so under **14** Chapter VII UN Charter, the UN Security Council has rarely formally decided on the existence of an act of aggression in a given case.[31] Thus, while the UN General Assembly, by adopting Resolution 3314 (XXIX), had attempted to provide for parameters for such a determination, States still could not agree on whether such an act had been properly defined in the said resolution, and further whether the definition, provided that were the case, was proper to be used for purposes of individual criminal responsibility (namely given the specific requirements of legal certainty in the field of [international] criminal law).

The second main challenge obviously related to the role of the UN Security Council **15** when it came to the determination of the existence, or not, of an act of aggression. Certain States were not in support of any role for the UN Security Council, certain States were in favour of a somewhat limited role, while yet others were in favour of the UN Security Council's complete role in its interaction with the Court for the purposes of investigating and prosecuting the crime of aggression. It would take until the very last minute to resolve the issue of the UN Security Council's role, particularly as this concerned its ability to determine an act of aggression, as well as its power to refer a situation of aggression to the ICC Prosecutor.

The inclusion of the crime of aggression faced significant challenges and took **16** many years. Eventually, of course, aggression found its way into the Rome Statute as one of the crimes within the Court's jurisdiction. Finally, on 14 December 2017, by Resolution ICC-ASP/16/Res.5, the Assembly of State Parties (ASP) decided to activate jurisdiction as of 17 July 2018 (exactly 20 years after the adoption of the Rome Statute).

3. History of outlawing aggression under international law

The topic of aggression has been covered under a wide range of international legal **17** instruments over the past century. In particular, these instruments have covered aggression within the contexts of individual criminal responsibility as well as State responsibility under international law.

---

[30] See *supra* mn. 8.
[31] Krisch, in: Simma *et al.* (eds.), *The Charter of the United Nations. A Commentary*, 3rd ed., 2012, Art. 39, mns. 42 *et seq.*; Strapatsas, in: Barriga and Kreß (eds.), *The Crime of Aggression: A Commentary*, 2017, 178.

a) League of Nations Covenant

18   The League of Nations, the predecessor of the UN, included within its Covenant reference to aggression. The Covenant, which was signed in 1919 and entered into force in 1920, provided under Article 10 the following:

> *"The Members of the League undertake to respect and preserve as against external aggression the territorial integrity and existing political independence of all Members of the League. In case of any such aggression or in case of any threat or danger of such aggression the Council shall advise upon the means by which this obligation shall be fulfilled."*

While the Covenant thus did indeed reference aggression, it however did not provide a definition.

19   Yet the League of Nations lasted only until 1946. Given the failure of the League of Nations in properly responding to World War II, it was dissolved and shortly replaced thereafter by the UN.

b) Kellogg-Briand Pact

20   The Kellogg-Briand Pact, or the "General Treaty for Renunciation of War as an Instrument of National Policy",[32] was signed in 1928 between France and the United States. The United States had not joined the League of Nations.

21   It was signed and ratified by 15 States, and later acceded to by an additional 48 States. While not referring specifically to aggression for various political reasons, Article I of the Pact provided that "[t]he High Contracting Parties solemnly declare in the names of their respective peoples that they condemn recourse to war for the solution of international controversies, and renounce it, as an instrument of national policy in their relations with one another".[33]

c) 1933 Convention for the Definition of Aggression

22   In 1933, the Convention for the Definition of Aggression[34] was adopted. This Convention was signed by Romania, Estonia, Latvia, Turkey, the USSR, Persia and Afghanistan. Finland later joined the Convention. It was primarily a treaty between the USSR and neighbouring countries.

23   According to the Convention, an "aggressor" was identified under Article II as a State committing one of the following acts:

> *"(1) Declaration of war upon another State;*
> *(2) Invasion by its armed forces, with or without a declaration of war, of the territory of another State;*
> *(3) Attack by its land, naval or air forces, with or without a declaration of war, on the territory, vessels or aircraft of another State;*
> *(4) Naval blockade of the coasts or ports of another State;*
> *(5) Provision of support to armed bands formed in its territory which have invaded the territory of another State, or refusal, notwithstanding the request of the invaded*

---

[32] See *supra* mn. 3.

[33] On the Kellogg-Briand Pact, see more generally Hathaway/Shapiro, *The Internationalists: How a Radical Plan to Outlaw War Remade the World*, 2017; Lesaffer, "Kellogg-Briand Pact (1928)", in: *MPEPIL*.

[34] 147 LNTS 67.

State, to take, in its own territory, all the measures in its power to deprive those bands of all assistance or protection."

Article III of the Convention explains that "[n]o political, military, economic or other 24 considerations may serve as an excuse or justification for the aggression referred to in Article 2". Examples of such excuses or justifications were included in an annex to the Convention. The first category of excuses or justifications was the "internal condition of a State". The examples falling under this category included "its political, economic or social structure; alleged defects in its administration; disturbances due to strikes, revolutions, counter-revolutions, or civil war". The second category included the "international conduct of a State", meaning "the violation or threatened violation of the material or moral rights or interests of a foreign State or its nationals; the rupture of diplomatic or economic relations; economic or financial boycotts; disputes relating to economic, financial or other obligations towards foreign States; frontier incidents not forming any of the cases of aggression specified in Article 2". As noted by the introductory paragraph to the annex, these examples were considered non-exhaustive.

d) International Military Tribunals

After the end of World War II, two international military tribunals were set up to 25 investigate and prosecute Axis Powers for crimes committed during the course of the war.

One was the International Military Tribunal, or the Nuremburg Tribunal. Article 6(a) 26 of the Charter of the International Military Tribunal provided the Tribunal jurisdiction over the crime of aggression:

"Crimes against peace: namely, planning, preparation, initiation or waging of a war of aggression, or a war in violation of international treaties, agreements or assurances, or participation in a common plan or conspiracy for the accomplishment of any of the foregoing"

The other was the International Military Tribunal for the Far East, or the Tokyo Tribunal. Article 5(a) of its Charter contained a virtually same worded provision.

Several individuals were held responsible by both tribunals for committing the crime 27 of aggression.[35]

e) UN Charter

Article 1 (1) of the UN Charter provides that one of the purposes of the UN is to 28 "maintain international peace and security, and to that end: to take effective collective measures for the prevention and removal of threats to the peace, and for the suppression of acts of aggression or other breaches of the peace". Art. 2 (4), the most central provision of the Charter, does not refer to aggression, but at least stipulates that "[a]ll Members shall refrain in their international relations from the threat or use of force against the territorial integrity or political independence of any state, or in any other manner inconsistent with the Purposes of the United Nations". Article 39 of the UN Charter in turn provides that "[t]he UN Security Council shall determine the existence

---

[35] See IMT, Judgment of 1 October 1946, in *The Trial of German Major War Criminals. Proceedings of the International Military Tribunal sitting at Nuremberg, Germany*, Part 22, 1950, 485 *et seq.*: The Nuremberg Tribunal sentenced 12 individuals: Rudolf Hess, Hermann Göring, Karl Dönitz, Wilhelm Frick, Walther Funk, Alfred Jodl, Wilhelm Keitel, Konstantin von Neurath, Erich Raeder, Joachim von Ribbentrop, Alfred Rosenberg and Arthur Seyss-Inquart; *Yuki, Tanaka et al., (eds.)* Beyond Victor's Justice? The Tokyo War Crimes Trials Revisited, 2010, 147 *et seq.*: The Tokyo Tribunal sentenced 8 individuals for crimes against peace.

of any threat to the peace, breach of the peace, or act of aggression and shall make recommendations, or decide what measures shall be taken in accordance with Articles 41 and 42, to maintain or restore international peace and security". Articles 41 and 42 include measures both involving and not involving the use of armed force which can be taken by UN Members under Chapter VII of the UN Charter. Furthermore, Article 53 of the UN Charter provides the UN Security Council with the power to authorize enforcement actions.

29   By way of Article 39 of the UN Charter, the UN Security Council may determine an act of aggression and decide on measures to be taken in response to such acts. Nevertheless, while the UN Security Council has made determinations on threats to peace and breaches of peace, it has only rarely used the term "act of aggression"; the last time it found that a State had committed an aggressive act was back in 1990 by Resolution 667.[36]

30   Article 51 of the UN Charter further provides that nothing within the Charter "shall impair the inherent right of individual or collective self-defence if an armed attack occurs against a Member of the United Nations, until the Security Council has taken measures necessary to maintain international peace and security". Thus, any attack taken under Article 51 would not constitute an act of aggression.

31   The UN Security Council has the primary responsibility of maintaining international peace and security, yet this is not exclusive. Where the UN Security Council fails in carrying out its primary responsibility, the UN General Assembly may take action.[37] Yet while the General Assembly has referred to aggression in numerous resolutions, it does not have powers under Chapter VII of the UN Charter, as the UN Security Council decides on measures to be taken in response to an act of aggression.

32   Like the League of Nations Covenant, the UN Charter does not define aggression as such. Years later, the UN General Assembly would take on the task of defining aggression.

f) UN General Assembly "Definition of Aggression"

33   In 1974, the UN General Assembly adopted Resolution 3314 (XXIX), which included within its annex a definition of aggression. Thereby the UN General Assembly attempted to provide guidance for the UN Security Council. According to para. 4 of the resolution, the UN General Assembly called "the attention of the Security Council to the Definition of Aggression, as set out below, and recommends that it should, as appropriate, take account of that Definition as guidance in determination, in accordance with the Charter, the existence of an act of aggression".

34   Resolution 3314 defined aggression as "the use of armed force by a State against the sovereignty, territorial integrity or political independence of another State, or in any other manner inconsistent with the Charter of the United Nations, as set out in this Definition".

35   It further identified a series of non-exhaustive acts which, according to the UN General Assembly, qualify as an act of aggression. These acts included the following:

> *"(a) The invasion or attack by the armed forces of a State of the territory of another State, or any military occupation, however temporary, resulting from such invasion or attack, or any annexation by the use of force of the territory of another State or part thereof;*
>
> *(b) Bombardment by the armed forces of a State against the territory of another State or the use of any weapons by a State against the territory of another State;*

---

[36] Strapatsas, in: Barriga and Kreß (eds.), *The Crime of Aggression: A Commentary*, 2017, 178, 180; Krisch, in: Simma *et al.* (eds.), *The Charter of the United Nations. A Commentary*, 3rd ed., 2012, Art. 39, mns. 42 *et seq.*

[37] UN Doc A/RES/377, *Uniting for Peace* Resolution, 3 November 1950.

(c) The blockade of the ports or coasts of a State by the armed forces of another State;

(d) An attack by the armed forces of a State on the land, sea or air forces, or marine and air fleets of another State;

(e) The use of armed forces of one State which are within the territory of another State with the agreement of the receiving State, in contravention of the conditions provided for in the agreement or any extension of their presence in such territory beyond the termination of the agreement;

(f) The action of a State in allowing its territory, which it has placed at the disposal of another State, to be used by that other State for perpetrating an act of aggression against a third State;

(g) The sending by or on behalf of a State of armed bands, groups, irregulars or mercenaries, which carry out acts of armed force against another State of such gravity as to amount to the acts listed above, or its substantial involvement therein."

Furthermore, Article 5 (2) of the said resolution provided that "[a] war of aggression **36**
is a crime against international peace" and that "[a]ggression gives rise to international responsibility".

As further explained within the text, while the definition of the crime of aggression **37**
proved to be a key divisive issue between States for its inclusion within the Rome Statute, it was eventually adopted based on the acts delineated by Resolution 3314.

g) Draft Code of Crimes against the Peace and Security of Mankind

In 1996, the ILC adopted the Draft Code of Crimes against the Peace and Security of **38**
Mankind.[38] The Draft Code would serve as the predecessor for the Rome Statute of the ICC.

Article 2 (2) of the Draft Code provided that "[a]n individual shall be responsible for **39**
the crime of aggression in accordance with article 16". Article 16, titled the "Crime of aggression", stipulated that "[a]n individual who, as leader or organizer, actively participates in or orders the planning, preparation, initiation or waging of aggression committed by a State shall be responsible for a crime of aggression".

Nevertheless, as explained below, States could not come to an agreement on the **40**
inclusion of the crime of aggression within the Rome Statute and the Draft Code did not properly include a definition for States to work with.

h) Articles on the Responsibility of States for Internationally Wrongful Acts

In 2001, the ILC adopted the Articles on Responsibility of States for Internationally **41**
Wrongful Acts (ARSIWA),[39] including a norm on *"jus cogens"* violations.

Article 26 provides the rule that States cannot preclude the wrongfulness of an act **42**
"which is not in conformity with an obligation arising under a peremptory norm of international law". According to the commentaries to Article 26, the ILC cited the ICJ *East Timor* case, identifying the prohibition of aggression as a peremptory norm of international law.

Article 40 further covers international responsibility of a State "which is entailed by a **43**
serious breach [...] of an obligation arising under a peremptory norm of generally international law". The commentaries also allude to the prohibition of aggression as a

---

[38] ILC, *Draft Code of Crimes Against the Peace and Security of a Mankind*, 48ᵗʰ. Sess., July 1996, UN Doc. A/CN.4/L.522 and Corr. 1.
[39] ILC, *Draft Articles on Responsibility of States for Internationally Wrongful Acts*, November 2001, Supplement No. 10 (A/56/10), chp.IV.E.1.

peremptory norm. Prior to the adoption of the articles, the ILC had identified what it referred to as "international crimes". While this concept did not find its way into the final version, aggression was identified as falling within this category.

4. Structure

44   This manuscript on the crime of aggression as covered by the Rome Statute of the ICC is broken down into several sections. It covers the legal history of its inclusion into the Rome Statute and subsequently analyses the relevant articles as they stand today – Articles 8 *bis*, 15 *bis* and 15 *ter* of the Rome Statute. These particular provisions cover: the definition of the crime of aggression; the exercise of jurisdiction over the crime of aggression through State referrals and the *proprio motu* powers of the ICC Prosecutor; and the exercise of jurisdiction over the crime of aggression through UN Security Council referrals respectively. As such, the structure of this book will follow the structure of these three particular provisions, while also covering their relationship to other relevant articles of the Rome Statute as well as related issues under international law.

45   Part 2 deals with the crime of aggression under the Rome Statute prior to the amendments made in the 2010 Review Conference in Kampala, Uganda. Up until the adoption of the Rome Statute for the ICC, this included the works of the ILC, the Preparatory Committee, as well as the discussions of the 1998 Rome Conference. In particular, it analyses the debates surrounding the two most contentious issues, being the definition of aggression as well as the possible role of the UN Security Council in relation to the ICC. It is followed by the post-Rome Conference developments and, in particular, the work of the Special Working Group on the Crime of Aggression (SWGCA) established by the ASP to the Rome Statute of the ICC.

46   Part 3 in turn covers the definition of the crime of aggression and the underlying act of aggression post-2010 Review Conference in Kampala (Article 8 *bis* of the Rome Statute). The section first looks into the origins of the definition adopted in Kampala, although a significant part of this section is already covered by part 2. It then goes into the definition of an *act* of aggression, as well as the varieties of such acts listed within; before then moving on to the definition of a *crime* of aggression providing for international criminal responsibility. This is followed by an analysis of both, the relevant provisions of the Rome Statute as they pertain to the actual perpetrators of the crime, and of the relationship of the crime of aggression amendments with other parts of the Rome Statute.

47   Part 4 then looks at the aggression-related treaty based jurisdiction (Article 15 *bis* of the Rome Statute). In particular, this concerns the Court's ability to exercise its jurisdiction through State referrals and the *proprio motu* powers of the ICC Prosecutor. It analyses the Court's jurisdiction *ratione temporis*, or the temporal jurisdiction of the Court. It also addresses the conditions that were necessary to actually activate the Court's aggression-related jurisdiction, after the required 30 States parties had ratified the crime of aggression amendments, plus the required vote by two-thirds of the States parties of the Rome Statute. It also looks at the challenges faced in terms of the ability for States to "opt-out" of the Court's jurisdiction over the crime of aggression. Finally, this part covers the Court's interaction with the UN Security Council with regards to the crime of aggression, and the ability for the ICC Prosecutor to proceed without a determination of the UN Security Council.

48   Part 5 then deals with the UN Security Council-based jurisdiction. In particular, this part analyses the specific role of the UN Security Council in its ability to refer situations directly to the ICC Prosecutor.

Finally, part 6 covers the crime of aggression and the ICC post-2017. This concludes **49**
with the future of the Court's ability to exercise jurisdiction over the crime of
aggression. It addresses the various challenges after the Court's jurisdiction has been
activated – in particular as well as the significant challenges faced by the three ways in
which the Court may exercise such jurisdiction (State referral, *proprio motu*, or by way
of UN Security Council referral).

The Appendix includes a number of annexes, being relevant excerpts from the Rome **50**
Statute; resolutions and understandings adopted at the 2010 Review Conference in
Kampala; the UN General Assembly Resolution on the Definition of Aggression of 1974
(which served as a basis for Article 8 *bis* of the Rome Statute). Each of these documents
are referenced throughout the text of this book.

II.
THE CRIME OF AGGRESSION UNDER THE ROME STATUTE
PRIOR TO THE KAMPALA AMENDMENTS

Article 5 (1) (d) of the Rome Statute, as agreed upon in Rome in 1998, stipulates that **51** the Court shall – apart from genocide, crimes against humanity and war crimes – also have jurisdiction with respect to the crime of aggression. However, the former Article 5 (2) read:

> *"The Court shall exercise jurisdiction over the crime of aggression once a provision is adopted in accordance with articles 121 and 123 defining the crime and setting out the conditions under which the Court shall exercise jurisdiction with respect to this crime. Such a provision shall be consistent with the relevant provisions of the Charter of the United Nations."*

Up until its eventual inclusion into the Rome Statute, aggression had been a key, **52** divisive issue for States. In particular, the most contentious aspects of aggression were on the definition of the crime and the various aspects concerning the possible role of the UN Security Council. With regards to the crime of aggression, the amendments (to be adopted subject to the regular procedure provided for in Articles 121 and 123[40]) were supposed to provide for a definition, while also setting out the conditions under which the Court can exercise jurisdiction with respect to the crime.

Eventually, the crime of aggression found its way into the Rome Statute of the ICC during the Review Conference held in Kampala, Uganda between 31 May and 11 June 2010, by adding Articles 8 *bis*, 15 *bis* and 15 *ter* to the Rome Statute (and by deleting Article 5 (2)).

Over 7 years later, on 14 December 2017, the ASP activated the Court's jurisdiction **53** over the crime as of 17 July 2018 (*i. e.* exactly 20 years after the adoption of the Rome Statute).

Until the entry into force of the amendments, the crime of aggression was thus *de* **54** *facto* not yet included in the Statute – its status as a crime under customary international law notwithstanding.[41] One question that might have arisen was whether the UN Security Council might have explicitly granted the Court the competence to exercise its jurisdiction with respect to the crime of aggression at any given moment and with regard to a specific situation, given its overriding powers under Chapter VII of the UN Charter and the supremacy of the Charter pursuant to its Article 103 (and notwithstanding Article 5 (2) of the Rome Statute). Yet, given that Article 15 *ter* of the Rome Statute now specifically regulates the exercise by the Court of its UN Security Council-based jurisdiction with regard to the crime of aggression, that question was to be answered in the negative.

---

[40] See the comments by Clark, in: Triffterer/Ambos, *The Rome Statute of the International Criminal Court*, 3rd ed., 2016, Art. 121 and 123; Zimmermann, 10 *JICJ* 2012, 209 *et seq.*

[41] See for such proposition the judgment of the British *House of Lords* of 29 March 2006 in *R. v. Jones*, where the *House of Lords* held that aggression is indeed criminalized under international customary law, 45 *ILM* 2006, 992.

1. The debate leading up to the "non-inclusion" of the crime of aggression in the Rome Conference

55 Efforts towards the crime of aggression's inclusion in the Rome Statute of the ICC can be found in the works prepared by the ILC, the so-called Preparatory Committee as well as during the discussions of the 1998 Rome Conference. Yet at the end of the Rome Conference, the Rome Statute was complete with the crime of aggression serving as a mere "placeholder" for its future consideration due to the inability of States to agree on its substance.

a) Draft Code submitted by the International Law Commission

56 In 1996, the UN's ILC adopted the *Draft Code of Crimes against the Peace and Security of Mankind*. In its *Draft Code*, the ILC identified several categories of crimes, including: the crime of aggression, the crime of genocide, crimes against humanity, crimes against UN and associated personnel, as well as war crimes. While the ILC did indeed include the crime of aggression, it made no attempt towards a workable definition of the crime.[42]

57 In an earlier draft prepared by the ILC, the *Draft Code* had included a provision under which any proceedings by the ICC in dealing with an act of aggression, or connected therewith, could not be initiated unless the UN Security Council had previously made a determination that the State in question had indeed committed such an act.[43] Under Chapter VII of the UN Charter, the UN Security Council has the power to determine whether or not an act of aggression, threat to peace or breach of peace has taken place. To date, the UN Security Council has rarely determined on that an act of aggression has taken place.[44] For a number of reasons, many States were not in favour of this approach.

b) Discussions during the Preparatory Committee

58 After the ILC submitted the *Draft Code* to the UN General Assembly, the latter created the "Preparatory Committee on the Establishment of an International Criminal Court", with a mandate to prepare a draft statute for the future ICC. The discussions held with the Preparatory Committee, concerning both the definition of the crime of aggression, as well as the role for the UN Security Council, demonstrated the deep divisions that existed among delegations and the States that they represented.

aa) Definition of the crime of aggression

59 As for the definition of the crime of aggression itself, there were two main schools of thought. One group of countries, including a large number of Arab as well as African States, favoured an approach which was largely based on the definition contained in UN General Assembly Resolution 3314 (XXIX) of 14 December 1974 titled "*Definition of Aggression*", by which the UN General Assembly had undertaken an attempt to define aggression.[45] According to Article 1 of Resolution 3314, "[a]

---

[42] *YbILC* Vol. II, Part 2 1995, 38–39.

[43] Article 23 (2) of the ILC Draft Statute 1994.

[44] Strapatsas, in: Barriga and Kreß (eds.), *The Crime of Aggression: A Commentary*, 2017, 178; Krisch, in: Simma *et al.* (eds.), *The Charter of the United Nations. A Commentary,* 3ʳᵈ ed., 2012, Art. 39, mns. 42 *et seq.*

[45] For details see UN DOC A/CONF.183/C.1/L.37, 1 July 1998, and A/CONF.183/C.1/L.56, 8 July 1998.

ggression is the use of armed force by a State against the sovereignty, territorial integrity or political independence of another State, or in any other manner inconsistent with the Charter of the United Nations, as set out in this Definition". Article 3 (a-g) of Resolution 3314 sets out a series of acts qualifying as an act of aggression, while Article 4 explains that the list is non-exhaustive. However, this seemed to be problematic since it was rather doubtful that all of the elements contained in Resolution 3314 can be considered as forming part of customary international law.[46] Nevertheless, as noted, Resolution 3314 included a definition of the crime, as well as several acts that would amount to aggression.

Resolution 3314 itself was drafted in order to serve as a guiding instrument for the **60** UN Security Council to make such a determination under Chapter VII of the UN Charter which would, in turn, invoke the responsibility of a State in committing such an act. Even assuming *arguendo* that this provision is reflective of customary international law, it would still be doubtful as to whether all of the acts of aggression contained within Resolution 3314 already *de lege lata* involve individual criminal responsibility. This is confirmed by the fact that the first principle of the UN General Assembly's *Declaration on Principles of International Law concerning Friendly Relations and Co-operation among States in accordance with the Charter of the United Nations*,[47] as well as Article 5(2) of Resolution 3314, provide that solely the waging of a "war of aggression" constitutes a crime which entails responsibility in accordance with international law – but not every act which is supposed to have been outlawed by the text of the resolution. At the same time the *Friendly Relations Declaration* provides that "[a] war of aggression constitutes a crime against the peace, for which there is responsibility under international law". Article 5 (2) of Resolution 3314 similarly provides that "[a] war of aggression is a crime against international peace. Aggression gives rise to international responsibility".

On the other hand, a majority of countries involved in the negotiation process – and **61** in particular Germany which was very active in trying to move the discussion forward[48] – attempted to present a definition of the crime of aggression which would be both, precise and narrowly tailored. The objective was to limit individual criminal responsibility to clear-cut cases of the illegal and massive use of armed force leading to the invasion of foreign territory, relying itself on the few existing precedents and, specifically, on Article 6(a) of the Statute of the Nuremberg Military Tribunal, which stipulated that the "planning, preparation, initiation or waging of a war of aggression, or a war in violation of international treaties, agreements or assurances, or participation in a common plan or conspiracy for the accomplishment of any of the foregoing" constitutes a crime against peace".[49]

bb) Role of the UN Security Council

A similar split amongst States surfaced as to the role and function of the UN Security **62** Council with regard to the prosecution of individuals for future instances of aggression. On the one hand, the United States proposed that the definition of the crime of aggression should include a formula according to which the illegality of the act under

---

[46] See *ICJ, Military and Paramilitary Activities in and against Nicaragua (Nicaragua v. United States of America)*, Judgement (Merits), ICJ Rep. 1986, 14, 103, para. 195, where the Court stated that Article 3 (g) of Resolution 3314 "may be taken to reflect customary international law".

[47] UN DOC A/RES/2625 (XXV), 24 October 1970.

[48] See the statement made by the then German Minister of Foreign Affairs Kinkel, *NJW* 1997, 2860 *et seq.*

[49] As to the German approach see in particular UN DOC A/AC.249/1997/WG.1/DP.20, 11 December 1997; A/AC.249/1998/DP.12, 1 April 1998, and finally A/AC.249/1998/CRP.8, 2 April 1998.

consideration would be determined by the UN Security Council.[50] On the other hand, those countries favouring a broad definition of the crime of aggression envisaged no role whatsoever for the UN Security Council. As a compromise, the proposal of the ILC[51] seems to have been favoured by quite a number of States. Yet, as was the case with the definition of the crime of aggression, this question was not resolved during the work of the Preparatory Committee.

c) Discussions during the Rome Conference

63   The Preparatory Committee was followed by the United Nations Conference of Pleni-potentiaries on the Establishment of an International Criminal Court in 1998, or the "Rome Conference". At the Rome Conference, the same two issues – the definition of the crime as well as the role of the UN Security Council – re-emerged as divisive issues during the debate on the inclusion of the crime of aggression into the Rome Statute. With the conclusion of the Rome Conference, no compromise could be reached on either of the two issues.

64   First, no generally acceptable definition of the crime of aggression could be agreed upon. In particular, States from the Arab and African regions of the world continued to insist on a rather wide definition largely based on UN General Assembly Resolution 3314 – and even going beyond that definition.[52] On the other hand, Germany continued its efforts to come up with a proposal which could be both in line with relevant precedents and which could serve as a basis for a compromise between both sides.[53]

65   Second, although not extensively dealt with during the Rome Conference due to both, a lack of time and a missing solution for the definition of the crime of aggression, the role of the UN Security Council also remained controversial. A proposal from Camer-oon provided that, once an alleged perpetration of the crime of aggression had been submitted to the ICC, the ICC would be under an obligation to refer the matter to the UN Security Council for a determination as to whether or not an act of aggression had taken place.[54] In case the UN Security Council failed to make such a determination within a reasonable time, the ICC would then be entitled to commence an investigation. This proposal was not discussed in much detail.

66   Due to the lack of a generally accepted formula in both regards, a Bureau proposal submitted to the Rome Conference on 10 July 1998[55] did not contain any reference to the crime of aggression. Instead, it simply stipulated that the crime of aggression might be referred to a future "Review Conference". A proposal submitted by the members of the Non-Aligned Movement[56] then provided for the inclusion of the crime of aggression but that the definition of the crime – somewhat similar to the former Article 5 (2) of Resolution 3314 – should be elaborated upon by the Preparatory Commission and later adopted by the ASP. The Preparatory Commission was established by Resolution F of the Final Act of the Rome Conference.

---

[50] See the proposals contained in Preparatory Committee, Decisions, 14 August 1997, A/AC.249/1997/L.8/Rev.1, p. 7, https://iccnow.org/documents/DecisionsTaken14Aug97.pdf (last accessed May 2019); Zimmermann, 2 *M.P. Y.B.UN. L.* 1998, 202.

[51] *Supra* mns. 56 *et seq.*

[52] For details see UN DOC A/CONF.183/C.1/L.37, 1 July 1998, and A/CONF.183/C.1/L.56, 8 July 1998. See also the proposal submitted by Armenia (UN DOC A/CONF.183/C.1/L.38, 1 July 1998) which wanted to include a specific exception for those cases of armed attacks "required by the principle of equal rights and self-determination of peoples".

[53] See also the proposals submitted by Cameroon, UN DOC A/CONF.183/C.1/L.39, 2 July 1998, under which any manifestly illegal use of armed force would have constituted a crime of aggression.

[54] UN DOC A/CONF.183/C.1/L.39, 2 July 1998.

[55] UN DOC A/CONF.183/C.1/L.59, 10 July 1998.

[56] UN DOC A/CONF.183/C.1/L.75, 14 July 1998.

It was against this background that the Bureau of the Rome Conference included the   **67**
compromise text that became Article 5 (2) in the final version of the Rome Statute.
Article 5 (2) of the Rome Statute eventually provided that "[t]he Court shall exercise
jurisdiction over the crime of aggression once a provision is adopted[...]defining the
crime and setting out the conditions under which the Court shall exercise jurisdiction
with respect to this crime".

d) Post-Rome developments

The discussion on the future inclusion of the crime of aggression then continued   **68**
within the framework of the Preparatory Commission for the ICC and, subsequently,
the ASP.

aa) Discussions in the framework of the Preparatory Commission for the International Criminal Court

The Preparatory Commission for the ICC, set up by the Final Act of the Rome   **69**
Conference, decided to create a working group on the crime of aggression. However,
the Preparatory Commission was not able to reach a consensus on the still out-
standing issues of the definition of the crime and the specific role of the UN Security
Council.

With regard to the first issue, most of the States involved maintained their previous   **70**
positions relating to the definition of the crime of aggression.[57] However, with regard to
the second issue on the role that the UN Security Council should play with regard to the
crime of aggression, two new options were submitted.

One option – if adopted – would have provided that the UN Security Council would   **71**
be requested by the Court as to whether in a given situation the crime of aggression has
been committed.[58] In the absence of a decision of the UN Security Council within a
given period of time, the Court could then proceed with its investigations or prosecution.

An alternative proposal – basing itself on UN General Assembly Resolution 377 (the   **72**
well-known *Uniting for Peace* Resolution) – provided that, if the UN Security Council
was not able to exercise its primary responsibility in maintaining international peace
and security and reach any such determination within a given time frame, the UN
General Assembly would then be asked in turn by the Court to make such a
recommendation.[59] Again, in a situation where no such recommendation were to be
made in due course, the Court could still go forward with its proceedings (under the
proposal as then submitted).

The working group also considered proposals for the possible elements of crimes   **73**
concerning the crime of aggression; however, the elements were not thoroughly
discussed. The Preparatory Commission finally submitted a report to the first session
of the ASP, where – basing itself on the work of the above-mentioned working group –
it outlined the various options submitted and discussed.[60]

bb) Discussions in the framework of the Assembly of States Parties

During its first session, the ASP in turn decided to create the SWGCA which –   **74**
given the overall importance of the issues involved – was open not only to States

---

[57] For an overview see notably PCNICC/2001/L.3/Rev.1, 11 October 2001.
[58] PCNICC/2001/L.3/Rev.1, Option 1, variation 1, p. 15, 11 October 2001.
[59] *Ibid.*, variation 2.
[60] PCNICC/2002/2/Add.2, 24 July 2002.

parties to the Rome Statute, but rather to all UN member States.[61] The SWGCA was tasked to submit proposals to the ASP for its consideration at the future Review Conference.

75   Neither during the first nor the second session of the ASP was any relevant progress made. The work of the SCGCA was then still being based on the option paper elaborated upon by the Preparatory Commission.[62]

76   The third session of the ASP, which took place from 6–10 September 2004, once again took note of the report of the SWGCA[63] without taking any further action.[64] The said working group held an inter-sessional meeting in June 2004, where it had considered the more technical aspects of aggression without going into the core issues outlined above (definition and role of the UN Security Council) where, in view of the participating States, significant progress was unlikely to take place.[65] In particular, the SWGCA considered issues related to: the exercise of jurisdiction *ratione temporis*; the possible incorporation and placement of a future provision on aggression; issues of complementarity and admissibility with regard to the crime of aggression; the principle of *ne bis in idem*; and finally the relationship of a possible provision on the crime of aggression with general principles of criminal law.

77   In 2005, the SWGCA continued its work, including by holding informal inter-sessional meetings, where once again the same issues were discussed.[66]

78   During the informal inter-sessional meeting of the SWGCA that took place in June 2006,[67] and as noted by the fifth meeting of the ASP,[68] the definition of the conduct of the individual concerned was one of the main issues. Following the Nuremberg precedent, a broad movement emerged towards *per se* limiting the individual criminal responsibility to those persons planning, preparing, initiating or executing the crime of aggression, thereby underlying the leadership character of the crime of aggression. Yet, with regard to the very definition of the crime of aggression, there continued to be significant debate. This debate centred around the question whether the list of acts contained in UN General Assembly Resolution 3314 should indeed serve as a basis for the definition of the crime of aggression, and whether a qualifying element should be added, such as *e.g.* referring to "manifest" or "grave" violations of the prohibition of the use of force.[69]

79   In 2007, the SWGCA continued its work.[70] Not the least, and apart from continuing its work with regard to the issues just mentioned, it also focused on the controversial relationship between the Court on the one hand and the UN Security Council on the

---

[61] Continuity of work in respect of the crime of aggression ICC-ASP/1/Res.1, 9 September 2002.

[62] As to details see ICC-ASP/1/3, 3–10 September 2002, ICC-ASP/1/3/Add.1, 3–7 February and 21–23 April 2003 (in particular ICC-ASP/1/L.4 – Proposal by Cuba, 6 February 2003), as well as ICC-ASP/2/10, 8–12 September 2002, para. 44 and Annex II.

[63] See ICC-ASP/3/25, 6–10 September 2004, para. 41.

[64] See ICC-ASP/3/25, 6–10 September 2004, para. 41.

[65] ICC-ASP/3/SWGCA/INF.1, para. 5.

[66] See as to details ICC-ASP/4/32, 28 November – 3 December 2005, para. 31.

[67] ICC-ASP/5/SWGCA/INF.1, 5 September 2006.

[68] ICC-ASP/5/35, 29 January – 1 February 2007, para. 19.

[69] It is worth noting that the International Court of Justice in the *Case concerning Armed Activities on the Territory of the Congo* (*Democratic Republic of the Congo v. Uganda*) referred to "[t]he unlawful military intervention by Uganda [...] of such a magnitude and duration that the Court considers it to be a grave violation of the prohibition of the use of force expressed in Article 2, paragraph 4, of the Charter", ICJ Rep. 2005, 168, para. 165. See also Separate Opinion of Judge Simma, *ibid.*, 334, para. 2, which qualified such behaviour as an "act of aggression".

[70] For details see Report of the Special Working Group on the Crime of Aggression, ICC-ASP/5/35, 29 January – 1 February 2007, as well as the report on its 2007 informal inter-session meeting, ICC-ASP/6/SWGCA/INF.1, 25 July 2007.

other with regard to the crime of aggression, an issue also already addressed to some extent in Article 5 (2) of the Rome Statute.

In February 2009, the SWGCA submitted its final report to the ASP. This report was **80** forwarded to the Review Conference that was to be held in Kampala in 2010.[71] The proposal contained a draft definition of the crime of aggression in the form of a proposed Article 8 *bis*, to follow the other three categories of crimes. However, no consensus was reached regarding the role of the UN Security Council in the exercise of jurisdiction over the crime of aggression (which is now addressed in Article 15 *bis*). Two versions of this draft provision were presented with varying options as to the role of the UN Security Council.[72] Accordingly, the requirements necessary for the ICC to exercise its jurisdiction over the crime of aggression was the most debated issue moving towards the Review Conference planned for Kampala in 2010.

2. Developments during the Kampala Review Conference

The SWGCA's definition of the crime of aggression was adopted *verbatim* at the 2010 **81** Review Conference.[73] The only additions to the definition were the elements of crimes[74] and certain "understandings" (further discussed below) as to the content of the "threshold" clause. Most of the debate that took place at the Review Conference centred around the preconditions for the Court exercising its jurisdiction with regard to the crime of aggression. As mentioned previously,[75] many alternatives had been proposed for Article 15 and the ensuing debate finally resulted in the creation of two articles, namely Articles 15 *bis* and 15 *ter*. Article 15 *bis* deals with State referrals and the ICC Prosecutor's *proprio motu* exercise of jurisdiction with regard to the crime of aggression, while Article 15 *ter* deals specifically with UN Security Council referrals.[76]

3. Preconditions for the exercise of the Court's jurisdiction over the crime of aggression and the legality of the amendment

The Court is only able to exercise its jurisdiction over purported crimes of aggression **82** now that the amendment adopted at the Review Conference actually has entered into force.[77] On 14 December 2017, the ASP decided to active the Court's jurisdiction over the crime of aggression as of 17 July 2018.

Article 5 (2) of the Statute, as adopted in Rome (and deleted in Kampala), provided **83** that the definition of the crime of aggression must be in line with the relevant provisions of the UN Charter. This reference to the UN Charter thereby, first and foremost, took into account the fact that under Article 103, any definition of the crime must stay within the limits provided by the Charter itself and accordingly, *inter alia*, had to recognize the legality of military action either authorized by the UN Security Council under Chapter VII of the UN Charter or undertaken in the exercise of the right

---

[71] ICC-ASP/7/SWGCA/2, 19 February 2009, the proposals can also be found in Annex II of the Resolution ICC- ASP/8/Res. 6, 26 November 2009.

[72] ICC-ASP/8/Res. 6, Annex II, 26 November 2009.

[73] ICC-ASP/RC/11, 31 May – 11 June 2010, Res. 6.

[74] ICC-ASP/RC/11, 31 May – 11 June 2010, Res. 5.

[75] See *supra* mns. 69 *et seq.*

[76] See *infra* mns. 273 and 402.

[77] As to details of the amendment and review procedure under Articles 121 and 123 see generally Clark, in: Triffterer/Ambos, *The Rome Statute of the International Criminal Court,* 3rd ed., 2016, Art. 121 and 123, and specifically with regard to the crime of aggression *ibid. passim.*

of self-defence (individual and collective) under Article 51 of the UN Charter.[78] Article 103 of the UN Charter specifically provides that "[i]n the event of a conflict between the obligations of the Members of the United Nations under the present Charter and their obligations under any other international agreement, their obligations under the present Charter shall prevail".

84   Besides, Article 5 (2) of the Rome Statute further stipulated that any provision shall also set out the conditions under which the Court shall exercise jurisdiction with respect to this crime, which in turn was supposed to be consistent with the relevant provisions of the UN Charter. This formula was used in order to address the question which role the UN Security Council should play for purposes of criminal proceedings involving the prosecution of instances of the crime of aggression. The Rome Statute, by stating explicitly that such a provision must be in line with the UN Charter, thereby seems to have acknowledged the special role and prerogatives that the main political organs of the organization, and first and foremost the UN Security Council (but also touching upon the role of the UN General Assembly), possess when it comes to the maintenance of international peace and security under Articles 12, 14, 24 and generally Chapter VII of the Charter.[79]

85   It is certainly true that any determination by the Court that the crime of aggression has been committed in a given case would solely focus on the criminal responsibility of one or more individual offenders eventually responsible for having committed such crime. It would not deal with issues of State responsibility and the maintenance of international peace and security as such.

86   Yet, any such determination by the Court will necessarily contain, provided the person concerned acted as organ of a State within the meaning of Article 4 of the ILC's ARSIWA, an implicit determination that the State on behalf of which the individual was acting, committed an act of aggression. Thus, by the same token, the said State was simultaneously under an obligation to make reparation for such act under the rules of international law governing the responsibility of States.

87   Besides, one might not exclude a situation where the UN Security Council, acting under Chapter VII of the UN Charter, either determines that a given State had not committed an act of aggression, but that it had rather been acting either in self-defence or within the framework of a valid UN Security Council authorization, or that such action, while constituting a breach of peace, did not yet amount to an act of aggression.

88   Even where any such express positive or negative determination by the UN Security Council is lacking, the accused could still claim that he or she acted (as was indeed argued by the United States and the United Kingdom in the case of the military action against Iraq in 2003) within the parameters of a UN Security Council authorization in which case the Court would eventually be faced with the task to consider the legality of the military action under general international law.

89   It is against the background of such scenarios that one has to evaluate the legality under both the UN Charter itself and Article 5 (2) of the Rome Statute, of the amendment regulating the exercise of jurisdiction by the Court with regard to the crime of aggression.

90   The amendment adopted in Kampala enables the Court to judge upon alleged acts of aggression without a prior determination by the relevant organs of the UN. It could thus

---

[78] As to questions concerning the use of armed force arising under Article 51 UN Charter see Randelzhofer, in: Simma *et al.* (eds.), *The Charter of the United Nations. A Commentary*, 3rd ed., 2012, Art. 51.

[79] For a detailed discussion see already Zimmermann, 2 *M.P. Y.B.UN. L.* 1998, 202 *et. seq.*

indeed, be it only implicitly and eventually *ex post facto*, subject to either the action of the organization or that of individual States acting under the authority of the UN (or both) and to the control of the Court (the ICC itself not being an organ of the UN).[80] Accordingly, it could eventually endanger the effectiveness of the system of collective security set up under the UN Charter.

The situation is thus comparable to the one addressed by the European Court of Human Rights in *Behrami and Sahramati*.[81] There, the Grand Chamber of the European Court of Human Rights similarly determined that any form of outside judicial control of action (even if the acts as such were undertaken by individual member States or a group of member States) which is crucial to the effective fulfilment by the UN Security Council of its Chapter VII mandate under the UN Charter and consequently, by the UN *in toto* of its imperative peace and security aim, would in itself interfere with the fulfilment of the UN's key mission in this field[82] and should thus be considered not admissible. **91**

Accordingly, it is submitted that in order to be in line with the requirements of the UN Charter and Article 5 (2) of the Rome Statute itself, an amendment on the crime of aggression should have contained safeguards. Such safeguards would have made sure that the Court would not prosecute an individual for the crime of aggression without either a prior determination by the relevant organs of the UN confirming that the underlying action by the State concerned amounted to an act of aggression, or without those UN organs specifically granting the Court jurisdiction over the crime of aggression.[83] **92**

Indeed, under Article 24 of the UN Charter, it is the UN Security Council that bears the primary responsibility for the maintenance of international peace and security. Under the UN Charter, it would therefore be primarily for the UN Security Council to eventually determine, acting under Chapter VII of the UN Charter, whether an act of aggression was indeed committed or grant the Court jurisdiction over the crime of aggression. **93**

Yet, this responsibility may not necessarily be exclusive to the UN Security Council. As confirmed by the ICJ in its Advisory Opinion on the *Legal Consequences of the Construction of a Wall in the Occupied Palestinian Territory*,[84] the competences of the UN Security Council, while being of a primary nature in that regard, are not necessarily exclusive.[85] More specifically, the ICJ confirmed that the accepted practice of the UN General Assembly when acting under the *Uniting for Peace* Resolution, as it has since evolved, is consistent with Article 12 (1) of the UN Charter.[86] The *Uniting for Peace* Resolution provides that: **94**

---

[80] The situation is thus significantly and indeed fundamentally different from any form of legal evaluation respectively control of acts of the Security Council or the General Assembly by either the International Court of Justice, the latter itself being the principal judicial organ of the United Nations, or by an *ad hoc* tribunal established by the Security Council itself under Chapter VII as one of its subsidiary organs within the meaning of Article 29 of the Charter.

[81] *Behrami vs. France*, Application No. 71412/01 and *Saramati vs. France, Germany and Norway*, Application No. 78166/01, Decision of 2 May 2007.

[82] *Ibid.*, para. 149. It should be also noted that the *European Court of Human Rights expressis verbis* extended its argument to attempts to control or limit voluntary acts of individual States such as the vote of a permanent member of the Security Council in favour of a Chapter VII Resolution, *ibid.*

[83] See for such a proposal Blokker, 20 *Leiden JInt'lL* 2007, 867 (889).

[84] *ICJ, Legal Consequences of the Construction of a Wall in the Occupied Palestinian Territory*, Advisory Opinion, ICJ Rep. 2004, 136, para. 26.

[85] *Ibid.*

[86] *Ibid.*, para. 28. As a matter of fact the General Assembly has on several occasions qualified certain acts as "aggressive acts", "acts of aggression" or "aggression", see for a detailed overview Blokker, 20 *Leiden JInt'lL* 2007, 867 (881).

"[…] if the Security Council, because of lack of unanimity of the permanent members, fails to exercise its primary responsibility for the maintenance of international peace and security in any case where there appears to be a threat to the peace, breach of the peace, or act of aggression, the General Assembly shall consider the matter immediately with a view to making appropriate recommendations to Members for collective measures, including in the case of a breach of the peace or act of aggression the use of armed force when necessary, to maintain or restore international peace and security."

95   Thus, any amendment of the Rome Statute circumscribing the conditions under which the Court may exercise its jurisdiction with regard to the crime of aggression could have also enabled the UN General Assembly to then eventually render the necessary decisions. This is, of course, provided that the procedural prerequisites as provided for in the *Uniting for Peace* Resolution are fulfilled. Naturally, it would be necessary to determine that the UN Security Council was unable to exercise its above-mentioned primary responsibility for the maintenance of international peace and security due to the exercise of the veto.

4. Outlook

96   In the lead-up to the 2010 Review Conference, there had been a few attempts to include other crimes within the jurisdiction of the Court. Such examples included attempts by certain States of including terrorism and drug-trafficking as well as the use of nuclear weapons. Yet, as expected, these crimes were not even seriously considered during the Kampala review process for a number of reasons. It is also safe to reason that future additions to the Rome Statute will neither deal with those nor similar "treaty crimes".

97   In contrast thereto, the issue of whether or not the crime of aggression was to be included into the Rome Statute constituted the major issue addressed during the 2010 Review Conference; and, if so, under what conditions. During the Review Conference, the outcome of which will be analysed in detail in the contributions dealing with Articles 8 *bis*, 15 *bis* and 15 *ter* specifically below, the following main results were reached:
– defining the individual conduct confirming the leadership character of the crime of aggression;
– clarifying the relationship with the general principles of criminal law as contained in the Rome Statute and particularly Article 25 (3);
– defining the underlying conduct of the State concerned; and
– delimiting the conditions for the exercise of jurisdiction with respect to the crime of aggression.

98   Given the difficulties encountered both before and during the Rome Conference, as well as during the work of both the Preparatory Commission as well as the SWGCA of the ASP, reaching consensus on certain issues had seemed to be a difficult obstacle to surmount; these issues being: a generally acceptable definition of the crime of aggression; delimiting the appropriate role of the UN Security Council; and further taking into account the threshold for an amendment to the Rome Statute. However, the Review Conference's inclusion of the crime of aggression raises a significant number of issues related to international treaty law, as well as that of the UN Charter.

99   Only time will tell what effects the amendment might have on the international system at large. Indeed, one might wonder whether the ambitious attempt to provide for

the jurisdiction of the Court with regard to the crime of aggression, not taking into account the role of the UN Security Council, might eventually overburden the Court. However, given the recent limit that was effectively set to the Court's jurisdiction (as planned in Kampala) by the 2017 activation decision,[87] maybe the actual threat constitutes rather an "underburdening" of the Court.

Furthermore, it might be a dangerous illusion to believe that the current imperfections of the international system, with the composition and voting mechanism of the UN Security Council clearly being a major one of them,[88] could be revised or challenged through the backdoor of the system of international criminal law.[89]

---

[87] See infra at mns. 359 *et seq.*

[88] See Zimmermann, in: Simma *et al.* (eds.), *The Charter of the United Nations. A Commentary* 3rd ed., 2012, Art. 27, mns. 265 *et seq.*

[89] See for such proposition Fife, in: Bergsmo (ed.), *Human Rights and Criminal Justice for the Downtrodden – Essays in Honour of Asbjørn Eide,* 2003, 54 (73).

III.
DEFINITION OF THE CRIME OF AGGRESSION AND THE UNDERLYING ACT OF AGGRESSION

The definition of the crime of aggression is now to be found in Article 8 *bis* of the **100** Rome Statute. Article 8 *bis* consists of three parts. Article 8 *bis* (1) defines the "crime of aggression", consisting of an "act of aggression" which, "by its character, gravity and scale, constitutes a manifest violation of the Charter of the United Nations". This is followed by Article 8 *bis* (2), which then defines such an "act of aggression"[90] by largely referring to the wording of UN General Assembly Resolution 3314 (XXIX) of 14 December 1974.[91] The chapeau of Article 8 *bis* (2) accordingly sets out the notion of an "act of aggression" in a generic manner, while Article 8 *bis* (2) (a)-(g) goes on to list the specific types of such acts. Finally, Article 8 *bis* (1) also defines the various modalities of the crime of aggression, as well as circumscribes who might commit any such crime of aggression.

Under the Kampala amendment, the first sentence of Article 9 (1) now also provides **101** that the Elements of Crimes, as adopted by the ASP at the Review Conference, shall assist the Court in the interpretation and application of Article 8 *bis* on the crime of aggression. The respective elements of crimes relating to Article 8 *bis* were adopted as Annex II of Resolution RC/Res. 6. They have accordingly been incorporated into the overall elements of crimes without any specific issues arising as to their legal relevance and impact on the interpretation of Article 8 *bis*.[92]

1. The origins of the definition adopted in Kampala

While the drafting history of Article 8 *bis* prior to the Review Conference has already **102** been discussed,[93] it is worth noting that the main debates concerning the crime of aggression that took place focused on the conditions for the Court's exercise of its jurisdiction. In particular, the Kampala negotiations focused on the respective role of the UN Security Council. This stands in contrast to the fact that no changes occurred during the 2010 Review Conference *vis-à-vis* the substance of the definition of the crime of aggression, which was adopted *verbatim* as already contained in the proposal by the SWGCA.[94]

While the 2010 Review Conference did not bring along discussions on the definition **103** of aggression itself or on the Elements of Crimes (of which a complete draft text was already existent)[95], the President's First Paper reflected progress on the drafting of the two Understandings related to the substance of the crime of aggression, namely Under-

---

[90] Also see Ambos, 53 *GYbIL* 2010, 463 (482), who differentiates between the "micro level" of the individual crime (para. 1) and the "macro level" of the collective State act of aggression (para. 2).

[91] UN DOC A/RES/29/3314 (XXIX), 14 December 1974, Annex: Definition of Aggression.

[92] See generally on the normative relevance and impact of the elements of crimes adopted under Article 9 Gadirov and Clark, in: Triffterer/Ambos (eds.), *The Rome Statute of the International Criminal Court*, 3rd ed., 2016, Art. 9, *passim*.

[93] See *supra* mns. 51 *et seq.*

[94] ICC-ASP/8/Res. 6, 26 November 2009.

[95] Anggadi, French and Potter, in: Barriga and Kreß (eds.), *The Travaux Préparatoires of the Crime of Aggression*, 2012, 58 (59).

standings no. 6 and 7, which aim to further define the content and substance of the crime.[96]

2. Definition of an act of aggression and its varieties

104   This section reviews the definition of an "act of aggression" as included within Article 8 *bis* (2) of the Rome Statute, as well as the types of acts within that article. It is necessary to first identify the act of aggression in order to qualify the crime of aggression in the second step.[97]

a) Definition of an "act" of aggression

105   According to Article 8 *bis* (2) of the Rome Statute:

> *"For the purpose of paragraph 1, "act of aggression" means the use of armed force by a State against the sovereignty, territorial integrity or political independence of another State, or in any other manner inconsistent with the Charter of the United Nations. Any of the following acts, regardless of a declaration of war, shall, in accordance with United Nations General Assembly resolution 3314 (XXIX) of 14 December 1974, qualify as an act of aggression [...].*"

106   Both the *chapeau* of, as well as the list of acts amounting to acts of aggression contained in Art 8 *bis* (2), mirror the wording of Articles 1 and 3 of UN General Resolution 3314 ("*Definition of Aggression*") as adopted in 1974. The definition of aggression contained in the said resolution, as confirmed by operative paragraph 4 of the resolution, aimed at guiding the UN Security Council, when making a determination on the existence of an act of aggression within the meaning of Article 39 of the UN Charter. Article 39 of the UN Charter provides that "[t]he Security Council shall determine the existence of any threat to the peace, breach of the peace, or act of aggression and shall make recommendations, or decide what measures shall be taken in accordance with Articles 41 and 42, to maintain or restore international peace and security." Notwithstanding, the SWGCA nevertheless supported its adaption to the context of criminal responsibility, an aspect which has been somewhat heavily criticized.[98]

107   The introductory words of Article 8 *bis* (2) confirm that the definition of what constitutes an act of aggression under this very paragraph is only meant to be relevant in order to find out whether or not a crime of aggression within the meaning of Article 8 *bis* (1) has been committed. In line with Understanding no. 4,[99] neither Article 8 *bis* (2) nor indeed Article 8 *bis*, *in toto*, are meant to have a direct impact on general international law in line with Article 10 which stipulates that "[n]othing in this Part shall be interpreted as limiting or prejudicing in any way existing or developing rules of international law for purposes other than this Statute".

aa) The "act" of aggression within the meaning of the UN Charter

108   As confirmed by the list of examples now forming part of Article 8 *bis* (2), an "act of aggression" requires a lower degree of gravity than the notion of an "armed attack"

---

[96] President's First Paper, 10 June 2010, in: Barriga and Kreß (eds.), *The Travaux Préparatoires of the Crime of Aggression*, 2012, 774. For the drafting process of the Understandings, also see Kreß, Barriga, Grover and von Holtzendorff, in: Barriga and Kreß (eds.), *The Travaux Préparatoires of the Crime of Aggression*, 2012, 81 (91 *et seq.*). For details on the respective Understandings and their drafting details, see mn. 243 *et seq.*

[97] See mns. 104 *et seq.*

[98] Heinsch, 2 *GoJIL* 2010, 713 (723).

[99] See *infra* mn. 203.

within the meaning of Article 51 of the UN Charter. As a matter of fact,[100] short-term military actions, while already arguably amounting to an act of aggression, do not necessarily constitute an armed attack (or indeed a crime of aggression) as defined in Article 8 *bis*.

Article 8 *bis* aims primarily at upholding the general prohibition of the use of force, **109** as contained in Article 2 (4) of the UN Charter, which prohibits both the threat and use of force generally. By using the formula "use of *armed* force", the wording of Article 8 *bis* (2) embraces a more restrictive approach than Article 2 (4) of the UN Charter, the wording of which refers to the "use of force" in general (as well as the threat of force, which in any event would exceed the adequate subject of criminalization given the current status of customary law on the matter).[101] Hence undeniably, political or economic force is not covered by Article 8 *bis*.[102] It ought to be noted, however, that even the scope of Article 2 (4) of the UN Charter is limited to the use of military force, as confirmed by para. 7 of the preamble of the UN Charter, as well as by Article 44 thereof, and, finally, by the UN General Assembly's *Friendly Relations Declaration*.[103]

As already indicated by Article 8 *bis* (1) ("by a person in a position effectively to **110** exercise control over or to direct the political or military action *of a State*")[104], Article 8 *bis* (2) clarifies for good that an act of aggression in the sense of this provision can only be committed by a State, not by private actors.[105] Accordingly, leaders and high-rank members of paramilitary or terrorist groups cannot be culpable of the crime of aggression with respect to acts committed by those groups. The prosecution of such private individuals under such circumstances remains entirely within the States' domestic jurisdiction.

Under certain circumstances, the commission of armed force by private actors can **111** nevertheless be attributable to a State under the regular rules of State responsibility, as codified in the ILC's ARSIWA[106] and, in particular, Article 8 thereof. Accordingly, the "effective control standard", as developed by the ICJ in its *Nicaragua* judgment, and more recently confirmed in its judgment on the merits in the *Bosnian Genocide* case, applies in order to eventually determine whether an act of aggression, even when committed by private actors, is nevertheless attributable to a State and thus constitutes "the use of armed force by a State" within the meaning of Article 8 *bis* (2).[107]

Furthermore, in line with such possible attribution of responsibility, a specific form of **112** such "indirect" use of force by a State is then referred to in Article 8 *bis* (2)(g) as one possible act of aggression.[108]

The formula contained within Article *8 bis* (2) – "against the sovereignty, territorial **113** integrity or political independence of another State, or in any other manner inconsistent with the Charter of the United Nations" – largely resembles the wording of Article 2 (4) of the UN Charter. This is with the exception that in line with Article 1 of UN General Assembly Resolution 3314, the words "against the sovereignty" were added and that the

---

[100] See *infra* mn. 240.
[101] Kreß and von Holtzendorff, 8 *JICJ* 2010, 1179 (1190).
[102] Broms, 154 (I) *RdC* 1977, 299 (342).
[103] UN DOC A/RES/25/2625, 24 October 1970; as to further details see Randelzhofer and Dörr, in: Simma *et al.* (eds.), *The Charter of the United Nations: A Commentary*, 3rd ed., 2012, Art. 2 (4), mns. 17 *et seq.*
[104] See mn. 221 *et seq.*
[105] Sayapin, *The Crime of Aggression in International Criminal Law*, 2014, 260.
[106] UN DOC A/56/83, 12 December 2001.
[107] See mns. 169 *et seq.*
[108] See mns. 166 *et seq.*

words "inconsistent with the purposes of the United Nations" were replaced by the words "inconsistent with the Charter of the United Nations". While, with regard to UN General Assembly Resolution 3314, the addition of "sovereignty" resulted from the focus of the newly independent (former colonial) countries on their sovereignty, the term "inconsistent with the Charter of the United Nations" was meant to cover also formal provisions of the UN Charter, such as those of Chapter VII.[109]

114   These words must however not be read in any way to imply that the provision is meant to only cover those instances of the use of military force which are directed against or aim at altering or abolishing another State's sovereignty, territorial integrity or political independence.[110] As a matter of fact, the respective latter parts of the wording of both, Article 1 of the UN General Assembly Resolution 3314, and already beforehand the similar formula of "in any other matter inconsistent with Purposes of the United Nations" in Article 2 (4) of the UN Charter are meant to reconfirm the general character of the prohibition of the use of force.[111] The notion of "integrity" should be understood as "inviolability", prohibiting any kind of forcible trespassing involving the use of military force.[112]

115   The term "of another State" indicates that only situations involving two States are covered.[113] Neither mere intra-State conflicts, nor acts against private actors are encompassed unless, obviously, such acts, while being directed against non-State actors take place on the territory of another State. The term's position within the provision does not mean that the use of armed force "in any other manner inconsistent with the Charter of the United Nations" does not require an action directed against another State.

116   The applicability of Article 8 *bis* (2), as indeed the applicability of the prohibition of the use of force in general, does not depend on the *de facto* effectiveness of another State's sovereignty, or put otherwise the prohibition (and eventually the exposure to punishment under Article 8 *bis*) also encompasses the use of armed force against so-called "failed States".[114]

117   The last alternative "or in any other manner inconsistent with the Charter of the United Nations" serves to fill in possible gaps in the scope of application of Article 8 *bis* (2). At the same time, it ensures that the use of military force that is in line with the UN Charter, and in particular when justified as an exercise of the right to self-defence under Article 51 of the UN Charter, or when authorized by the UN Security Council under Chapter VII of the UN Charter, does not amount to an act of aggression.[115] At the same time, the more formalistic notion of the "Charter of the United Nations" in Article 8 *bis* (2) (in contrast to "the Purposes of the United Nations" formula, as used in Article 2 (4) of the UN Charter) indicates that also instances of the use of armed force allegedly in line with such purposes might amount to an act of aggression.[116]

---

[109] Bruha, *Die Definition der Aggression*, 1980, 114.

[110] Randelzhofer and Dörr, in: Simma *et al.* (eds.), *The Charter of the United Nations: A Commentary*, 3rd ed., 2012, Art. 2 (4), mn. 37.

[111] Randelzhofer and Dörr, in: Simma *et al.* (eds.), *The Charter of the United Nations: A Commentary*, 3rd ed., 2012, Art. 2 (4), mn. 37 and 39 (referring to the *travaux préparatoires* of Article 2 (4)).

[112] Randelzhofer and Dörr, in: Simma *et al.* (eds.), *The Charter of the United Nations: A Commentary*, 3rd ed., 2012, Art. 2 (4), mn. 37; Dinstein, *War, Aggression and Self-Defence*, 5th ed., 2011, 91.

[113] Broms, 154 (I) *RdC* 1977, 299 (342).

[114] Randelzhofer and Dörr, in: Simma *et al.* (eds.), *The Charter of the United Nations: A Commentary*, 3rd ed., 2012, Art. 2 (4), mn. 40; for further details see Geiß, *Failed States*, 2005, 123 *et seq.*

[115] Broms, 154 (I) *RdC* 1977, 299 (343).

[116] See also already *supra* mn. 113.

bb) The "acts" as contained within UN General Assembly resolution 3314

The phrase "[a]ny of the following acts" must be read as meaning "*all* of the following **118**
acts" rather than as "only the following acts", since the list of acts enumerated in
Article 8 *bis* (2) (just like the one in UN General Assembly Resolution 3314) was not
meant to be an exhaustive one.[117] Indeed, the chapeau of the 2nd sentence of Article 8 *bis*
(2) states that the provision has to be interpreted in accordance with Resolution 3314,
Article 4 of which in turn explicitly provides that "[t]he acts enumerated above are not
exhaustive and [that] the Security Council may determine that other acts [also]
constitute aggression under the provisions of the Charter". This is confirmed by the
drafting history of the UN General Assembly Resolution 3314, according to which the
list of acts of aggression laid down in Article 8 *bis* (a)-(g) (and accordingly now also the
list of acts contained in Article 8 *bis* (2)) was not intended as an exclusive and strict rule,
but rather as interpretation material for the UN Security Council.[118]

During the drafting process in the SWGCA of what is now Article 8 *bis*, there were **119**
proposals such as the one presented by Germany, which wanted to introduce a more
clearly defined narrow definition of what amounts to an act of aggression, restricting the
potential scope of such acts.[119] In the end, however, there was no majority for such
proposals. The majority of delegations in favour of the current text held, as summarized
in the Official Records of the SWGCA, that even "[a]cts other than those listed could
[…] be considered acts of aggression", provided that they were of a similar nature and
gravity to those listed and would satisfy the general criteria contained in the chapeau of
paragraph 2.[120]

While this open-ended character of the list of possible acts of aggression seems to be **120**
relatively unproblematic (and even necessary) in the context of UN Security Council
decisions under Article 39 of the UN Charter, this vagueness might conflict with the
criminal law principle of legality, as enshrined in Article 22.[121] However, it seems to be
generally acknowledged that the principle of legality has a narrower scope in international law as compared to domestic (criminal) law.[122] Accordingly, other clauses of
international criminal law comprise somewhat similar open-ended elements as well,
such as Article 3 of the ICTY Statute,[123] or specifically within the framework of the
Rome Statute itself, Article 7 (1)(k) which refers to "[o]ther inhumane acts of a similar
character intentionally causing great suffering, or serious injury to body or to mental or
physical health".[124] Notwithstanding, it is still recommendable to ensure that the notion
of what constitutes a crime of aggression (and accordingly also as a *conditio sine qua
non* what constitutes an act of aggression) is not expanded too extensively. Any other
possible acts of aggression not listed as such in Article 8 *bis* (2)(a)-(g) should accordingly be narrowly construed and may only be considered as such provided they possess
mutatis mutandis the same character and gravity as one or more of the acts listed.[125]

---

[117] For a different view, see Ambos, 53 *GYbIL* 2010, 463 (487).

[118] Broms, 154 (I) *RdC* 1977, 299 (355).

[119] Kreß, 20 *EJIL* 2009, 1129 (1136).

[120] ICC–ASP/6/20/Add.1, Assembly of States Parties to the Rome Statute of the International Criminal
Court, Resumed Sixth Session, New York, 2–6 June 2008, Official Records, Annex II, Report of the Special
Working Group on the Crime of Aggression, 14, para. 34.

[121] See generally Broomhall, in: Triffterer/Ambos (eds.), *The Rome Statute of the International Criminal
Court,* 3rd ed., 2016, Art. 22.

[122] Heinsch, 2 *GoJIL* 2010, 713 (724).

[123] "The International Tribunal shall have the power to prosecute persons violating the laws or customs
of war. Such violations shall include, *but not be limited to*: […]".

[124] Emphasis added; as to this provision see Hall and Stahn, in: Triffterer/Ambos (eds.), *The Rome
Statute of the International Criminal Court*, 3rd ed., 2016, Art. 7, mns. 95 *et seq.*

[125] Clark, 2 *GoJIL* 2010, 689 (696).

121 At the same time, as the first introductory provision of the Elements of Crimes pertaining to Article 8 *bis* confirms, "any of the acts referred to in Article 8 *bis*, paragraph 2, qualify as an act of aggression". Put otherwise, it must be assumed that any of the acts listed can, as a matter of principle, reach the threshold, as set out in Article 8 *bis* (1). Finding otherwise would not only run counter to the provision just quoted but also, and even more importantly, to the very structure of Article 8 *bis in toto*.

122 Finally, over time, the military operations of a State may fulfil one or even more of the alternatives listed in Article 8 *bis* (2) even if they, when they began, did not yet amount to an act of aggression.

123 In modern international law, a declaration of war does no longer constitute a necessary requirement for either the existence of an armed conflict, or indeed an act of aggression. It was already during the drafting process of the 1933 *Convention for the Definition of Aggression*[126] that the requirement of such a declaration had become obsolete, given that Article 2 (1) of the said treaty had referred to a declaration of war as one among several examples of acts of aggression, indicating its character as nothing but one specific form of aggression.

124 After World War II, declarations of war have become very rare. With the four Geneva Conventions of 1949,[127] such declarations have also lost their legal significance for purposes of international humanitarian law, since common Article 2 (1) of the four Geneva Conventions provides that the Conventions "shall apply to all cases of declared war or of any other armed conflict which may arise between two or more of the High Contracting Parties, even if the state of war is not recognized by one of them". Accordingly, it does not matter for purposes of Article 8 *bis* whether one or both parties refer to their use of military force eventually constituting an act of aggression as a mere "police operation", a "humanitarian" or "peacekeeping operation", or simply deny being involved in any such use of force in the first place.

125 It ought to be stressed, however, that the acts named in Article 8 *bis* (2)(a)-(g) do not constitute examples of *crimes* of aggression, but merely of *acts* of aggression. In order for such an act to also qualify as a crime of aggression coming within the jurisdiction of the Court, it therefore must also fulfil the additional conditions set out in Article 8 *bis* (1) with regards to individual criminal responsibility as well as falling within the meaning of a manifest violation of the UN Charter.[128]

b) Varieties of an act of aggression, based on UN General Assembly resolution 3314

126 The different varieties of possible acts of aggression are found in Article 8 *bis* (2)(a)-(g) of the Rome Statute.

aa) Invasion, attack, military occupation or annexation

"(a) The invasion or attack by the armed forces of a State of the territory of another State, or any military occupation, however temporary, resulting from such invasion or attack, or any annexation by the use of force of the territory of another State or part thereof"

127 Article 8 *bis* (2)(a) refers to the classic form of aggression, subdivided into the invasion, the attack, the military occupation or annexation of the territory of a foreign

---

[126] 147 LNTS 69.
[127] 75 UNTS 31; 75 UNTS 85; 75 UNTS 135; 75 UNTS 287.
[128] See infra at mns. 233 *et seq.*

State. This provision reflects customary international law.[129] At most, one can discuss whether the inclusion of military occupation and annexation was really necessary or is, at least partially, redundant given that both forms of aggression presuppose that an invasion or attack has previously taken place.[130]

An "invasion" requires that the aggressor State's armed forces illegally trespass **128** another State's frontiers, thereby breaching the principle of the inviolability of State borders.[131] It does not matter whether such an invasion then takes place by land forces, by way of a military operation via the sea, or by airborne troops. Classical examples of an invasion would be the invasion of Poland by German troops in September 1939, or the invasion of Kuwait by Iraqi armed forces in 1990.

The term "attack" describes "the act of falling upon with force or arms, of commen- **129** cing battle", "an offensive operation"; an onset or an assault.[132] Given the context within which the term "attack" is used in Article 8 *bis* (namely for purposes of the *jus ad bellum*), the *jus in bello* definition of "attack" as contained in Article 49 (1) of Additional Protocol I to the Geneva Conventions[133] (namely that "attack" means "acts of violence against the adversary, whether in offence or in defence") is irrelevant. At the same time, any such act must not necessarily amount to an armed attack within the meaning of Article 51 of the UN Charter,[134] in order for it to constitute an "attack" within the meaning of Article 8 *bis* (2). Rather, it is Article 8 *bis* (1) that would determine the necessary threshold so as for the act of aggression concerned in form of an "attack" to eventually even amount to a crime of aggression.

It ought to be also noted that any use of armed force in line with international law **130** and, in particular, either in exercise of the right of self-defence under Article 51 of the UN Charter, or by virtue of an authorization by the UN Security Council under Chapter VII of the Charter, does not constitute an "attack" within the meaning of Article 8 *bis* (2)(a).

In order for either an invasion or an attack to constitute an act of aggression for **131** purposes of UN General Assembly Resolution 3314, and accordingly now also for purposes of Article 8 *bis* (2)(a), it must (at least also) involve the armed forces of the invading respectively attacking State. The provision thus constitutes a *lex specialis* to the general rules of attribution, as having been codified in the ILC's ARSIWA. More specifically, for any form of invasion or attack carried out by "armed bands, groups, irregulars or mercenaries", those acts could eventually be (also) attributed to the sending State under Article 8 of the ILC's ARSIWA and are governed by Article 8 *bis* (2)(g).

For purposes of *jus in bello*, the "armed forces" of a party to an armed conflict (and **132** thus also of a State when it comes, as in then scenarios covered by Article 8 *bis*, to international armed conflicts) are defined in Article 43 (1) of Additional Protocol I to the Geneva Conventions as all organized armed forces, groups and units which are under a command responsible to that State for the conduct of its subordinates, regardless of whether they constitute land, naval or air forces. Given that this definition was not only adopted in 1977 – *i. e.* after UN General Assembly Resolution 3314 had been adopted – but also for purposes of *jus in bello*, it cannot, as such, be considered as authoritative when it comes to Article 8 *bis* (2)(a), but may serve as a helpful tool in

---

[129] Dinstein, "Aggression", in: *MPEPIL*, mn. 25; also indicated by *ICJ, Armed Activities on the Territory of the Congo (DRC v. Uganda)*, Separate Opinion of Judge Simma, ICJ Rep. 2005, 334, 335, para. 3.

[130] Broms, 154 (I) *RdC* 1977, 299 (348).

[131] Sayapin, *The Crime of Aggression in International Criminal Law,* 2014, 266.

[132] *Cf.* Oxford English Dictionary Online.

[133] 1125 UNTS 3.

[134] As to the threshold requirements for a use of force amounting to an armed attack see already mn. 240.

defining the group of persons, action of which is relevant to determine whether an invasion respectively an attack has taken place. In any event, given the object and purpose of the provision, namely to protect the attacked respectively the invaded State, the acts of any organs of a State which involve the use of military force are to be considered acts of "armed forces", such acts by non-organs being covered by Article 8 *bis* (2)(g).

133   In order to make a finding as to whether an act of aggression in the form of an "invasion" or "attack" has taken place, the Court will eventually have to make a finding as to whether (as might be claimed) the alleged aggressor State has a valid title to the territory concerned, or rather not. If the former were the case, there would be not an invasion or attack of the territory of another State, even if the said other State had effective control of such territory. Put otherwise, the provision does protect the sovereignty of the invaded or attacked State. In contrast thereto, where the attacked State only exercised *de facto* control over the territory, sovereignty however lying with the invading State, there would not be, as required, an invasion or attack of the territory of another State.

134   It is worth noting that the first part of Article 8 *bis* (2)(a) dealing with the invasion or attack of "the territory of another State" does not, unlike the latter part thereof, also refer to the invasion or attack of "the territory of another State or part thereof". It stands to reason, however, that it is the very act of invading or attacking a foreign State that amounts to an act of aggression as such, even if the aim is to "only" do so on a limited geographic basis.

135   Under Article 42 of the 1907 Hague Regulations, having codified customary law on the matter, (military) "occupation" refers to situations where a State's military forces exercise effective control and authority over the territory of another State.[135] In line with Article 49 (2) of the Fourth Geneva Convention, a situation of occupation may also arise where the said occupation (*i.e.* in the case of Article 8 *bis* the one which is the result of an invasion or attack) meets with no armed resistance.

136   The words "however temporary" confirm that even a temporary occupation, *i.e.* one which is limited in time, amounts to an act of aggression. Yet, in order to reach the threshold provided for in Article 8 *bis* (1), a certain minimum duration of the occupation is required so as to provide for a violation of the prohibition of the use of force serious enough to constitute a crime of aggression. This is true, in particular, where the occupation is not only limited in time, but also merely to the extent of a small border area.

137   Apart from the fact that the part of Article 8 *bis* (2)(a) dealing with occupation does not, contrary to the part dealing with annexation of territory, explicitly state that even a partial occupation (just like a partial annexation) amounts to an act of aggression, an interpretation of the provision in line with customary international law provides that this is the case, a possible *argumentum e contrario* nevertheless.

138   Under the terms of Article 8 *bis* (2)(a), the occupation must result from an "invasion" or "attack", and must thus be the result of a use of force in violation of international law. Thus, an occupation of foreign territory which came about as the result of an exercise of the right of self-defence does not, as such, constitute an act of aggression.[136] During the drafting of UN General Assembly Resolution 3314, the question as to

---

[135] Convention (IV) respecting the Laws and Customs of War on Land and its Annex: Regulations concerning the Laws and Customs of War on Land, in: Scott, *The proceedings of the Hague Conferences,* 1920, 621; also see *ICJ, Armed Activities on the Territory of the Congo (DRC v. Uganda),* ICJ Rep. 2005, 168, 230, para. 173.

[136] Bruha, *Die Definition der Aggression,* 1980, 246.

whether an "excessive defensive" occupation caused by the exercise of the right of self-defence, but lasting for several years (or even decades) after the initial exercise of such a right, constitutes an act of aggression, could not be agreed upon. Accordingly, the question was deliberately left open,[137] nor was it addressed again when Article 8 *bis* was drafted. However, an unreasonably long-lasting occupation might amount to an "excess" of self-defence, and might then, depending on the specific circumstances, constitute an act of aggression by and of itself.[138]

While, under the terms of Article 8 *bis* (2)(a), the invasion or attack must be directed **139** against the territory of a foreign State, the provision does not require the ensuing occupation to then necessarily also relate to the territory of another State. This is confirmed by the very text of Article 8 *bis* (2)(a), which refers to "any military occupation". As a matter of fact, as the case of Palestine demonstrates, even an inter-State armed conflict might lead to the occupation of territory which, at least at the time the occupation took place, did not form part of a foreign State, or later on did not possess that status anymore.

Finally, where the UN Security Council, like in the case of Iraq, *ex post facto* **140** legitimizes an occupation regime, even one created by a violation of the UN Charter,[139] this either does not constitute an occupation covered by Article 8 *bis* (2)(a) in light of its object of purpose, or at the very least such an occupation would then not amount to a violation of the UN Charter, and even less a manifest one, the illegality of the prior invasion or attack notwithstanding.

"Annexation" covers the forcible acquisition of a State's territory by another state in **141** violation of international law. Additionally, an annexation normally requires a previous effective occupation, combined with the intention to appropriate the territory permanently.[140] Under Article 8 *bis* (2)(a), any such annexation must be the result of the use of force.

In line with the practice of the UN Security Council, even acts of a State purporting to **142** extend its domestic laws to occupied territory and assimilating it to its own territory, while not formally "annexing" as such, might nevertheless amount to a (*de facto*) annexation[141] also covered by that part of Article 8 *bis* (2)(a) here under consideration. In particular, this might be true where an occupying power physically separates part of the occupied territory adjacent to its own territory from the remainder of the occupied territory and, at the same time, transfers its own population into that very part of the occupied territory, while eventually simultaneously clearing it from the indigenous population.[142]

bb) Bombardment or use of weapons

"(b) Bombardment by the armed forces of a State against the territory of another State or the use of any weapons by a State against the territory of another State"

The term "bombardment" describes any attack from land, sea, or air bases with heavy **143** weapons which – like artillery, shells, missiles, or aircraft – are capable of destroying

---

[137] Bruha, *Die Definition der Aggression,* 1980, 245 *et seq.*

[138] For the question whether an excessive exercise of the right of self-defence may generally amount to a manifest violation of the Charter of the United Nations, see mn. 255.

[139] UN DOC S/RES/1483, 22 May 2003.

[140] Hofmann, "Annexation", in: *MPEPIL*, mn. 1.

[141] Hofmann, "Annexation", in: *MPEPIL*, mn. 33; see *e.g.* UN DOC S/RES/497, 17 December 1981, para. 1: "[…] the Israeli decision to impose its laws, jurisdiction and administration in the occupied Syrian Golan Heights is null and void and without international legal effect".

[142] See for such proposition *ICJ, Legal Consequences of the Construction of a Wall in the Occupied Palestinian Territory*, Advisory Opinion, ICJ Rep. 2004, 136, 184, para. 121.

enemy targets at a greater distance beyond the specific battle lines.[143] In contrast to Article 8 *bis* (2)(a), Article *8 bis* (2)(b) encompasses cases which do not require the attacking State's armed forces to physically cross the border. The notion of "bombardment" against the territory of another State covers not only situations where the weapon system is located on the attacking State's territory, but also where such systems have already been deployed on the territory of the State being attacked.

144   Given that Article 8 *bis* (2)(b) criminalizes violations of the *jus ad bellum*, it does not (only) criminalize bombardments of certain protected persons or objects, deriving from the principles of proportionality and distinction inherent in the *jus in bello* and criminalized by various provisions of Article 8. Rather, the norm refers generally to bombardments of another State's territory in general.[144]

145   The further elements of the provision covering bombardments, namely that such bombardment is undertaken by "the armed forces of a State" and is further directed "against the territory of another State" are identical to the terms used in Article 8 *bis* (2) (a), reference to which is therefore made.[145]

146   The second alternative of Article 8 *bis* (2)(b) refers to the use of "any weapons". Accordingly, while during the drafting process of what was to become UN General Assembly Resolution 3314, it had been proposed to introduce a specific reference to weapons of mass destruction, those weapons were in the end only referred to in the fifth preambular paragraph of the said resolution. Article 8 *bis* in turn does not contain any such reference at all. However, the term "use of any weapons" is broad enough to include the different kinds of weapons of mass destruction.

147   As in the case of the first alternative of Article 8 *bis* (2)(b) referring to "bombardments", the use of weapons must be directed against another State.[146] It is worth noting, however, that the second alternative of Article 8 *bis* (2)(b) generally refers to "the use of any weapons by a State". This stands in contrast to the first alternative thereof, which requires the "bombardment by the armed forces of a State". It thus stands to reason that any such use of weapons therefore constitutes an act of aggression by the respective State, whenever the action involved can be attributed to the attacking State under general rules of the law of State responsibility, even when not emanating from the armed forces of this State as such.

cc) Blockade

> *"(c) The blockade of the ports or coasts of a State by the armed forces of another State"*

148   Article 8 *bis* (2)(c) criminalizes "[t]he blockade of the ports or coasts of a State by the armed forces of another State". The term "blockade" describes belligerent operations to prevent vessels from entering or exiting ports or coastal areas belonging to another nation. It can take various forms, such as interdiction operations by vessels, or by mining the access routes to harbours. While a blockade has always been a common measure of economic warfare and constitutes a violation of the State's territory, it can also be directed against the armed forces of another State, in order to prepare an invasion or to cut off the other State's troop supply.[147] Given that a blockade does not necessarily involve the actual use of armed force, it is Article 8 *bis* (2)(c) that raises in

---

[143] McDonald and Bruha, "Bombardment", in: *MPEPIL*, mn. 1.

[144] Sayapin, *The Crime of Aggression in International Criminal Law*, 2014, 267.

[145] See mns. 131 *et seq.* and mn. 139.

[146] For further details see mn. 139.

[147] Heintschel von Heinegg, "Blockade", in: *MPEPIL*, mn. 1; Sayapin, *The Crime of Aggression in International Criminal Law*, 2014, 268.

particular the question whether such operations would always reach the threshold provided form in Article 8 *bis* (1).[148]

Under international humanitarian law (once States have entered into an armed **149** conflict), a blockade is only prohibited if it has the sole purpose of starving the civilian population or denying it other objects essential for its survival, or if the damage to the civilian population is, or may be expected to be, excessive in relation to the concrete and direct military advantage anticipated from the blockade.[149] However, since Article 8 *bis* generally, and Article 8 *bis* (2)(c) in particular, do not criminalize violations of the *jus in bello*, but rather those of the of *jus ad bellum*, such restrictions do not apply. Rather, any blockade may constitute an act of aggression, even if it abided by the limitations set out in international humanitarian law.

The blockade must then have the effect of blocking access to either the ports or the **150** coasts of a State. Given that the provision uses both terms in the plural, it stands to reason that the blockade of one single port does not fulfil the necessary criteria in order to constitute a blockade within the meaning of Article 8 *bis* (2)(c), unless such port would provide for the only access to the coasts of the victim State, and would thus by the same token amount to a blockade of the coasts of such victim State.

Since the provision covers only the coastal part of a State's transportation system, **151** landlocked States are not protected. As a matter of fact, already when UN General Assembly Resolution 3314 was drafted, a proposal in the respective Special Committee aimed at introducing an equivalent for the barring of passage to the open sea, but a majority of States was not willing to expand the scope of what is now the equivalent provision in Article 8 *bis* (2)(c). While one might assume an exception for land-locked States (and therefore an act of aggression) in extreme cases, *e. g.* when a State cuts off all communication routes of another State[150] for purposes of State responsibility, no such analogy seems to be permissible, given the unequivocal wording of Article 8 *bis* (2)(c) in light of the first sentence Article 22 (2), which provides that "[t]he definition of a crime shall be strictly construed and shall not be extended by analogy".[151]

Article 8 *bis* (2)(c) once again requires that the blockade is being undertaken by the **152** term "armed forces" of the attacking State, and may thus be carried out by land, air or naval forces.[152]

dd) Attack on the land, sea or air forces, or marine and air fleets of another State

"(d) An attack by the armed forces of a State on the land, sea or air forces, or marine and air fleets of another State"

Article 8 *bis* (2)(d), which refers to "[a]n attack by the armed forces of a State on the **153** land, sea or air forces, or marine and air fleets of another State", is *mutatis mutandis* identical to Article 8 *bis* (2)(a), reference to which is therefore made.[153] Its special purpose consists in the protection of State positions abroad. At least for purposes of

---

[148] See mns. 233 *et seq.*

[149] Doswald-Beck (ed.), *San Remo Manual on International Law Applicable to Armed Conflicts at Sea,* 1995, Art. 102.

[150] Randelzhofer and Nolte, in: Simma *et al.* (eds.), *The Charter of the United Nations: A Commentary,* 3rd ed., 2012, Art. 51, mn. 24.

[151] For details see Broomhall, in: Triffterer/Ambos (eds.), *The Rome Statute of the International Criminal Court,* 3rd ed., 2016, Art. 22, mns. 36 *et seq.*

[152] Randelzhofer and Nolte, in: Simma *et al.* (eds.), *The Charter of the United Nations: A Commentary,* 3rd ed., 2012, Art. 51, mn. 24; see as to the notion of "armed forces" also mns. 131 *et seq.*

[153] See mns. 126 *et seq.*

Article 8 *bis* (2)(d) it is, however, only military facilities that are considered to constitute such protected positions, but not diplomatic missions and nationals.[154] On the other hand, the provision also applies to military positions of a State on disputed territory.[155] The term "fleets" was chosen carefully to indicate that an attack on commercial fishing vessels or civilian aircraft would not amount to an act of aggression within the meaning of Article 8 *bis* (2)(d).[156] Even less would then boarding and search operations against commercial vessels, regardless of their legality under international law, fulfil the criteria laid down in Article 8 *bis* (2)(d).

154   The 2003 judgment of the ICJ in the *Oil Platforms* case had left open whether "the mining of a single military vessel might be sufficient to bring into play the "inherent right of self-defence"" and would thus also constitute an armed attack.[157] Such determination is then in turn relevant for purposes of Article 8 *bis* (1), when it comes to the gravity of the act and in order to decide whether such operation would then also eventually amount to a crime of aggression.

155   It remains unclear whether the attack has to directly target such military positions (*e.g.* by shooting at a ship or killing its crew), or whether the provision also applies when the attack merely forcefully hinders a plane or a ship to follow its course.[158] At the very least, however, such latter operations will hardly ever fulfil the "character", "gravity", and "scale" criteria, as contained in Article 8 *bis* (1).[159]

156   Given its wording, which specifically relates to attacks "on the land, sea or air forces, or marine and air fleets of another State", Article 8 *bis* (2)(d) does not cover attacks on a State's objects stationed in outer space.[160] This is confirmed by the fact that UN General Assembly Resolution 3314 was adopted seven years after the Outer Space Treaty,[161] which leads to the conclusion that the drafters excluded space objects deliberately from the scope of application of the provision, and the same is true with respect to the 2010 Review Conference, which again could have easily included space objects into the definition of protected military "outposts".

ee) Violation of stationing agreements and unlawful extension of presence

"(e) The use of armed forces of one State which are within the territory of another State with the agreement of the receiving State, in contravention of the conditions provided for in the agreement or any extension of their presence in such territory beyond the termination of the agreement"

157   Article 8 *bis* (2)(e) stipulates that "[t]he use of armed forces of one State which are within the territory of another State with the agreement of the receiving State, in contravention of the conditions provided for in the agreement or any extension of their presence in such territory beyond the termination of the agreement" constitutes an act of aggression. The provision has been drafted not the least in the light of post-World War II practice of forming military alliances, which routinely provide for army installations of one State within other member States,[162] but which may be misused against either the

---

[154] Verdross and Simma, *Universelles Völkerrecht,* 3rd ed., 1984, 290, mn. 473.

[155] Randelzhofer and Nolte, in: Simma *et al.* (eds.), *The Charter of the United Nations: A Commentary,* 3rd ed., 2012, Art. 51, mn. 26, with reference to the Argentinian invasion on the Falkland Islands in 1982.

[156] Broms, 154 (I) *RdC* 1977, 299 (351).

[157] ICJ, *Oil Platforms, (Iran v. USA),* ICJ Rep. 2003, 161, 195, para. 72.

[158] Bruha, *Die Definition der Aggression,* 1980, 117.

[159] See mns. 233 *et seq.*

[160] Sayapin, *The Crime of Aggression in International Criminal Law,* 2014, 273.

[161] 610 UNTS 205.

[162] Broms, 154 (I) *RdC* 1977, 299 (352).

receiving State, or indeed for military action against a third State, thereby exposing the receiving State in turn then being the object of military counter-attacks.

The provision includes two specific forms of acts of aggression, the first being the use **158** of force in contravention of the specific conditions of the agreement providing for the stationing of troops, while the second encompasses the use of force after the armed forces should have already left the foreign territory due to the lapse or termination of the agreement.

With respect to the first alternative, namely "[t]he use of armed forces of one State **159** which are within the territory of another State with the agreement of the receiving State, in contravention of the conditions provided for in the agreement", it ought to be noted that it requires that the stationing forces are being "used", the French text using the term "l'emploi". This does not seem to imply, however, that such troops then have to necessarily use military force against the territorial State in the sense of an attack. On the other hand, the term "use of armed forces" implies that there must be some element of genuine coercion inherent in the behaviour of the troops of the sending State, a mere technical violation of a stationing agreement not amounting to the actual use of armed forces within the meaning of the provision.

In line with the text of the provision, the said armed forces must find themselves on **160** the territory of the receiving State with the agreement of the receiving State. Given the further wording, such "agreement" has to take the form of a treaty, as confirmed by both the English and the French text, first using the general wording "with the agreement"/"avec l'agrément", but then later referring to the conditions set out in the respective "agreement"/"accord".

With respect to the second alternative, namely the "extension of [the] presence [of **161** armed forces[163] of one State which are within the territory of another State with the agreement of the receiving State] beyond the termination of the agreement", it ought to be noted that, as the ICJ held in the *Armed Activities* case, an agreement "facilitat[ing] the orderly withdrawal of [...] foreign forces [...] carries no implication as to [their]... military presence having been accepted as lawful".[164] At most, the principle of *bona fide* might imply that States must be given a reasonable amount of time to withdraw their troops, once a stationing agreement has been terminated.[165]

ff) Allowing one's territory to be used for an act of aggression

"(f) The action of a State in allowing its territory, which it has placed at the disposal of another State, to be used by that other State for perpetrating an act of aggression against a third State"

Article 8 *bis* (2)(f) regulates a State assisting another State in perpetrating an act of **162** aggression by allowing its territory to be used by said other State to commit an act of aggression.

For one, the State must use the territory which was placed at its disposal to actually **163** commit an "act of aggression" against a third State within the meaning of Article 8 *bis* (2)(a)-(e), or (g).

Furthermore, given the fact that the territory must have been placed at the disposal of **164** the State undertaking the act of aggression, it is only the voluntary provision of territory that itself then constitutes an act of aggression. Accordingly, cases in which a State has

---

[163] As to the notion of armed forces see mns. 131 *et seq.*

[164] *ICJ, Armed Activities on the Territory of the Congo (DRC v. Uganda)*, ICJ Rep. 2005, 168, 210, paras. 97, 99.

[165] Randelzhofer and Nolte, in: Simma *et al.* (eds.), *The Charter of the United Nations: A Commentary*, 3rd ed., 2012, Art. 51, mn. 29.

unsuccessfully tried to prevent such misuse,[166] or in which the State has been illegally invaded and occupied itself by the aggressor State, which now uses the territory to commit acts of aggression against additional States, are not covered by Article 8 *bis* (2) (f). On the other hand, it does not matter whether the territorial State had placed its territory at the disposal of the State committing the act of aggression by way of a treaty, or otherwise.

165   As a matter of principle, it is obviously not prohibited to allow another State to use one's territory for the stationing of armed forces or the instalment of arms.[167] In order for the receiving State therefore to itself commit an act of aggression, it must be aware of the kind of use of its territory to be made by the primary aggressor State in order to itself then qualify as an aggressor State.[168] What is more is that the provision further requires that there must be some specific "action [...] in allowing its territory [...], which it has placed at the disposal of another State, to be used by that other State for perpetrating an act of aggression against a third State". Put otherwise, the conclusion of a stationing agreement by the host State without then taking any further steps towards allowing an act of aggression to take place does not yet fulfil the requirements underlying Article 8 *bis* (2)(f). This is confirmed by the drafting history of that part of UN General Assembly Resolution 3314 mirroring Article 8 *bis* (2)(f). In particular, the wording "with the acquiescence and agreement of the former" contained in a draft of the said resolution was substituted by the current wording, in order to exclude merely passive behaviour from the scope of Article 8 *bis* (2)(f).[169]

gg) Sending of irregular forces

"(g) The sending by or on behalf of a State of armed bands, groups, irregulars or mercenaries, which carry out acts of armed force against another State of such gravity as to amount to the acts listed above, or its substantial involvement therein"

166   Article 8 *bis* (2)(g) covers forms of "indirect" aggression by sending irregular forces of various kinds into another State to then carry out acts of armed force in such latter State. In accordance with Article 8 *bis* (1), it is then not the actual persons carrying out the acts of armed violence belonging to non-State armed groups that eventually commit a crime of aggression, but rather the persons controlling or directing the State policy of sending such irregular forces into another State.

167   While what is now Article 8 *bis* (2)(g) had been very controversial during the drafting process of what was to become UN General Assembly Resolution 3314, in its *Nicaragua* case and as later confirmed in the *Armed Activities on the Territory of the Congo* case, the ICJ considered it to constitute a reflection of customary international law.[170]

168   The term "sending" implies (and thus also requires) a sufficiently close link between the "sending" State and the non-State group actually carrying out the armed operations, so that the latter would then have to either be qualified as *de facto* organs of the sending State, or at least as being controlled by the "sending" State within the meaning of Article 8 of the ILC's ARSIWA.[171]

---

[166] Randelzhofer and Nolte, in: Simma *et al.* (eds.), *The Charter of the United Nations: A Commentary*, 3rd ed., 2012, Art. 51, mn. 30, with further references.

[167] Sayapin, *The Crime of Aggression in International Criminal Law*, 2014, 269.

[168] Broms, 154 (I) *RdC* 1977,299 (353).

[169] See Bruha, *Die Definition der Aggression*, 1980, 263.

[170] ICJ, *Military and Paramilitary Activities in and against Nicaragua (Nicaragua v. United States of America)*, Judgement (Merits), ICJ Rep. 1986, 14, 103, para. 195; also see ICJ, *Armed Activities on the Territory of the Congo (DRC v. Uganda)*, ICJ Rep. 2005, 168, 222, para. 146.

[171] Randelzhofer and Nolte, in: Simma *et al.* (eds.), *The Charter of the United Nations: A Commentary*, 3rd ed., 2012, Art. 51, mn. 33.

This triggers the question as to the necessary degree of control that is required to **169** equate the sending and conduct of the mentioned non-State actors – armed bands, groups, irregulars and mercenaries – with direct acts of the sending State under the said Article 8 of the ILC's ARSIWA. In its *Nicaragua* judgment, the ICJ held that such control must amount to "effective control". By "effective control", the Court meant a situation where the State directly controls the perpetration of specific acts.[172]

As is well-known, the Appeals Chamber of the International Criminal Tribunal for **170** the Former Yugoslavia (ICTY) contested the *Nicaragua* judgment's *effective control* test. In its *Tadić* case, the Tribunal argued that the *Nicaragua* test was inconsonant with both, the logic of the law of State responsibility and with judicial, as well as with State practice,[173] the required degree of control being one of "overall" control over subordinate armed forces or military or paramilitary units "going beyond the mere financing and equipping of such forces and involving also participation in the planning and supervision of military operations".[174]

In its 2007 judgment in the *Bosnian Genocide* case, the ICJ however rightly upheld **171** the position laid out in the *Nicaragua* judgment and plainly rejected the criticism brought up by the ICTY in the *Tadić* case. The Court argued that the overall control criterion was useful for concluding whether a State was involved in a conflict on another State's territory and hence whether a conflict was international, but underlined that the ICTY was not called upon to decide on questions of State responsibility.[175] Accordingly, in order for insurgents to having been sent "by or on behalf of a State" for purposes of Article 8 *bis* (2)(g), they must either qualify as *de facto* organs, or be within the effective control of the "sending" State.

For purposes of the *jus ad bellum* issue addressed in Article 8 *bis* (2)(g) "armed **172** bands" and "groups" do not seem to require a certain degree of organization and organizational coherence and hierarchy, such as a command structure and the capacity to sustain military operations. This is confirmed by an *argumentum e contrario* with Article 8 (2)(f), which unlike Article 8 *bis* (2)(g) here under consideration, refers to "organized" armed groups. The term "groups" should also encompass private military and security companies.[176]

"Irregulars" are understood as opposed to the term of "regular armed forces" as **173** used in international humanitarian law. Under Article 43 (1) of the Additional Protocol I to the Geneva Conventions, the armed forces of a State party to a conflict consist of all organized armed forces, groups and units which are under a command responsible to that party for the conduct of its subordinates, even if that party is represented by a government or an authority not recognized by an adverse party. In contrast, thereto, the term "irregular forces" comprises militia or voluntary corps[177], not subject to a formal chain of command and not forming part of the armed forces of a party to a conflict.

---

[172] ICJ, *Military and Paramilitary Activities in and against Nicaragua (Nicaragua v. United States of America)*, Judgement (Merits), ICJ Rep. 1986, 14, 64 *et seq.*, para. 115.

[173] ICTY, *The Prosecutor v. Duško Tadić*, No. IT-94-1, Judgment, Appeals Chamber, 15 July 1999, paras. 115–45.

[174] ICTY, *The Prosecutor v. DuškoTadić*, No. IT-94-1, Judgment, Appeals Chamber, 15 July 1999, para. 145.

[175] ICJ, *Application of the Convention on the Prevention and Punishment of the Crime of Genocide (Bosnia and Herzegovina v. Serbia and Montenegro)*, ICJ Rep. 2007, 43, 210, para. 404.

[176] Sayapin, *The Crime of Aggression in International Criminal Law*, 2014, 270.

[177] *Cf.* Convention (IV) respecting the Laws and Customs of War on Land and its Annex: Regulations concerning the Laws and Customs of War on Land, 18 October 1907, 36 Stat. 2277, TS No. 539, Regulation 1.

174 The term "mercenary" is defined in both, Article 47 of the Additional Protocol I to the Geneva Conventions and in Article 1 of the 1989 *International Convention against the Recruitment, Use, Financing and Training of Mercenaries*.[178] Accordingly, a mercenary is any person who is specially recruited locally or abroad in order to fight in an armed conflict; is motivated to take part in the hostilities essentially by the desire for private gain and, in fact, is promised, by or on behalf of a party to the conflict, material compensation substantially in excess of that promised or paid to combatants of similar rank and functions in the armed forces of that party; is neither a national of a party to the conflict nor a resident of territory controlled by a party to the conflict; is not a member of the armed forces of a party to the conflict; and has not been sent by a State which is not a party to the conflict on official duty as a member of its armed forces.

175 The third parties listed in Article 8 *bis* (2)(g), namely armed bands, groups, irregulars and mercenaries, are not meant to encompass single individuals (although the last two may theoretically do so) since they were supposed to commit acts similar in gravity to the one otherwise listed in Article 8 *bis* (2).[179]

176 The various actors just referred to (*i.e.* armed bands, groups, irregulars and mercenaries) must actually "carry out acts of armed force against another State of such gravity as to amount to the acts listed above", *i.e.* as listed in Article 8 *bis* (2)(a)-(f). Not only must they therefore use "armed force" as defined above,[180] but those acts must also be directed against a third State. Finally, such acts must be similar in gravity to the other acts mentioned in Article 8 *bis*. It is worth noting, however, that the comparison only relates to the gravity of their acts but not to their scale, or indeed their character.[181]

177 In contrast to the first alternative of Article 8 *bis* (2)(g), *i.e.* the "sending by or on behalf of a State", the second alternative, *i.e.* "[the State's] substantial involvement", pays tribute to the difficulties of providing evidence for the first alternative.[182] This second alternative is vaguer than the first one and has not yet been sufficiently addressed by international courts. In the *Armed Activities* case, the ICJ did not properly differentiate between these two alternatives of Article 3(g) of UN General Assembly Resolution 3314 (now reproduced in Article 8 *bis* (2)(g)), but merely indicated that this form of State aggression generally requires a careful assessment of the standard and burden of proof.[183]

178 As a matter of principle, allowing non-State actors to make use of one's territory in order to prepare for acts of aggression similar to those listed in Article 8 *bis* (2) against persons or property situated in another State may be considered as the respective host State's "substantial involvement" within the meaning of Article 8 *bis* (2)(g).[184] It remains doubtful, however, whether a mere failure to take repressive measures against such acts (be it for a lack of ability or willingness) ought to be already considered to give rise to a substantial involvement, and thus eventually even give rise to a punishment for a crime of aggression.

hh) Other forms of aggression not listed

179 Given that Article 8 *bis* (2) merely repeats the respective wording of UN General Assembly Resolution 3314, modern methods of warfare, such as the use of "cyber-

---

[178] 2163 UNTS 75.

[179] Broms, 154 (I) *RdC* 1977, 299 (354).

[180] See mn. 109.

[181] For the content of these three terms see mns. 53 *et seq.*

[182] Broms, 154 (I) *RdC* 1977, 299 (354).

[183] ICJ, *Armed Activities on the Territory of the Congo (DRC v. Uganda)*, ICJ Rep. 2005, 168, 222, para. 146.

[184] Sayapin, *The Crime of Aggression in International Criminal Law*, 2014, 260.

force", unforeseeable in 1974, but a major topic in modern international law,[185] have not been listed in Article 8 *bis* either. However, as shown above, the list of possible acts of aggression, as contained in Article 8 *bis* (2), is not exhaustive,[186] although any other acts should be interpreted narrowly and must equate the character of the acts listed in order to also amount to an act of aggression for purposes of Article 8 *bis* (2).

It is worth noting that in the context of the notion of "armed attacks" in the sense of   **180** Article 51 of the UN Charter, the ICJ has held that the exercise of the right to self-defence does not depend on the type of weapon employed for a given attack.[187] Still, it remains difficult to interpret this statement in a way that electronic measures could be treated as "weapons" in the sense of Article 8 *bis* (2)(b).[188] At the very least, methods of "cyber warfare" would have to bring about destructive effects comparable to those of conventional weapons, such as the disabling of the State's infrastructure[189] in order to constitute an act of aggression within the meaning of Article 8 *bis* (2).

c) Contentious cases of aggression

While there is no fixed "canon" of scenarios where the issue will most likely arise,   **181** whether a given military action will amount to a violation of the UN Charter, let alone a "manifest" one, issues of preventive/pre-emptive self-defence, self-defence against non-State actors operating from the territory of another State, humanitarian intervention, implicit authorizations and revitalization of previous UN Security Council resolutions, interventions upon invitation, as well as the rescue of one State's own nationals abroad will be among the most likely scenarios in which the issue of whether such uses of force amount to a manifest violations of the UN Charter will arise.

aa) Preventive and pre-emptive self-defence

Article 51 of the UN Charter provides that nothing in the Charter shall impair the   **182** inherent right of individual or collective self-defence, if an armed attack occurs against an UN Member, until the Security Council has taken measures necessary to maintain international peace and security. This definition has, ever since its incorporation into the Charter, given rise to a number of controversies.

For one, while the ICJ (and following its jurisprudence also the Ethiopian-Eritrean   **183** Claims Commission)[190] has held that the term of armed attack is narrower than the scope of Article 2 (4) of the UN Charter,[191] only the gravest forms of the use of force constituting armed attacks,[192] the matter has remained somewhat controversial.[193] This raises the question whether an armed response to a use of force, which is short of an armed attack within the meaning of the jurisprudence of the ICJ would then not only be

---

[185] See generally Schmitt (ed.), *Tallinn Manual on the International Law Applicable to Cyber Warfare*, 2013, *passim*.

[186] See *supra* mn 59.

[187] *ICJ, Legality of the Threat of Use of Nuclear Weapons*, Advisory Opinion, ICJ Rep. 1996, 226, 244, para. 39.

[188] For a different view, see Randelzhofer and Nolte, in: Simma *et al.* (eds.), *The Charter of the United Nations: A Commentary*, 3rd ed., 2012, Art. 51, mn. 43.

[189] Randelzhofer and Nolte, in: Simma *et al.* (eds.), *The Charter of the United Nations: A Commentary*, 3rd ed., 2012, Art. 51, mn. 43, with further references.

[190] See mn. 240.

[191] Randelzhofer and Nolte, in: Simma *et al.* (eds.), *The Charter of the United Nations: A Commentary*, 3rd ed., 2012, Art. 51, mn. 6.

[192] *ICJ, Military and Paramilitary Activities in and against Nicaragua (Nicaragua v. United States of America)*, Judgement (Merits), ICJ Rep. 1986, 14, 101, para. 191; *ICJ, Oil Platforms (Iran v. USA)*, ICJ Rep. 2003, 161, 186, para. 51.

[193] Wilmshurst, 55 *ICL* 2006, 963.

unlawful under the UN Charter, but rather also manifestly unlawful within the meaning of Article 8 *bis* (1).

184   If an armed attack occurs, the exercise of the right of self-defence must be both, necessary and proportionate. However, surpassing the threshold of necessity and proportionality will not automatically lead to a manifest violation of the UN Charter.

185   In contrast thereto, instances of alleged "pre-emptive" self-defence against a possible attack which is said to occur in the farer future, as, *inter alia*, alluded to in the United States National Security Strategy of 2002, which stipulated that the right of pre-emptive self-defence which would be legal "even if uncertainty remains as to the time and place of the enemy's attack",[194] would not only amount to a violation of the UN Charter as such, but also to a manifest one. This assumption is supported by the unequivocal reaction by the international community to Israel's bombing of the Iraqi nuclear reactor Osirak in 1981, and to the US-led invasion of Iraq in 2003.[195] At the very least, as of today, the ICJ has clarified in its judgment in the *Armed Activities* case between the DRC and Uganda that "Article 51 of the Charter may justify a use of force in self-defence only within the strict confines there laid down" and that "[i]t does not allow the use of force by a State to protect perceived security interests beyond these parameters" given that "[o]ther means are available to a concerned State, including, in particular, recourse to the Security Council".[196] Given this unequivocal 2005 statement by the principal judicial organ of the UN Charter, it stands to reason that any future instance of such alleged "pre-emptive" self-defence would amount to a "manifest" violation of the UN Charter.

bb) Self-defence against non-State actors

186   Self-defence against non-State actors, namely terrorist groups, operating from the territory of another State, remains a matter of dispute. For purposes of Article 8 *bis*, this raises the question whether the use of military force against such groups, when taking place in a third State (the "target State"), constitutes a manifest violation of the UN Charter.

187   If the target State itself can be held responsible for the acts carried out by such groups under regular rules of State responsibility, and further provided such terrorist acts are comparable to acts of regular armed forces, the right to self-defence would be triggered[197]. This would then in turn not only exclude a manifest violation of the UN Charter, but any such violation *tout court*.

188   Were this however not the case, *i. e.* in situations in which the acts of the non-state actor are not attributable to a State, the ICJ in its Advisory Opinion on the *Legal Consequences of the Construction of a Wall in the Occupied Palestinian Territory* found that the inherent right of self-defence only applies "in the case of armed attack by one State against another State".[198] This approach has however been challenged not only by the practice of the UN Security Council when adopting Resolution 1368 one day after the terrorist attacks of 9/11 in which it referred to "the inherent right of individual or collective self-defence in accordance with the Charter".[199] This was affirmed by Resolution 1373, as the UN Security Council, acting under Chapter VII, adopted several measures on international terrorism, obliging all states to "[t]ake the necessary steps to prevent the commission of terrorist

---

[194] http://georgewbush-whitehouse.archives.gov/nsc/nss/2002/nss5.html [last accessed May 2019].

[195] UN Doc S/RES/487 (19 June 1981); Sifris (2003) 4 *MelbJIL* 521, 537; also see mn. 194.

[196] *ICJ, Armed Activities on the Territory of the Congo (DRC v. Uganda)*, ICJ Rep. 2005, 168, 223, para. 148.

[197] Shaw, *International Law*, 7th ed., 2014, 823.

[198] *ICJ, Legal Consequences of the Construction of a Wall in the Occupied Palestinian Territory*, Advisory Opinion, ICJ Rep. 2004, 136, 194, para. 139, emphasis added.

[199] UN DOC S/RES/1368, 12 September 2001, preambular part, para. 3.

acts".[200] Moreover, the ICJ in its *Armed Activities* case between the DRC and Uganda left it deliberately open whether attacks emanating from non-State actors may trigger the right of self-defence[201]. Yet, there is at least some amount of State practice indicating that large-scale terrorist attacks, especially when originating from the territory of States which deliberately failed to prevent them, can amount to an armed attack in the sense of Article 51 of the UN Charter, hence triggering the right of self-defence.[202]

At the very least and given the current debate on the matter, it thus seems safe to **189** assume that the use of military force as a reaction to armed attacks emanating from non-State actors would at least not amount to a "manifest" violation of the UN Charter, as required by Article 8 *bis* (1) in order for such use of force to eventually constitute a crime of aggression.

cc) Humanitarian intervention/Responsibility to protect

In cases of massive human rights violations where the UN Security Council refuses to **190** authorize the use of force (or where it is foreseeable that a respective draft resolution would be vetoed), and where self-defence is not applicable either, it has been argued that the concept of humanitarian intervention may justify the use of force.[203] This concept is an attempt to legalize the use of armed force in, and directed against, a foreign state for the prevention or discontinuation of massive human rights violations. State practice referred to, in order to justify the legality of such behaviour, encompasses the interventions by India in Bangladesh (1971), Vietnam in Cambodia (1978), Tanzania in Uganda (1979), the United States in Grenada (1983) and, most prominently, NATO member States in Kosovo (1999).

However, one might doubt whether these examples do indeed fulfil the requirements **191** to provide for a new rule of customary international law, namely extensive and uniform state practice as well as sufficient *opinio iuris*,[204] even more so since both of the two interventions for primarily humanitarian reasons, the Indian invasion in Bangladesh,[205] as well as the NATO intervention in Kosovo,[206] were condemned by a majority of States, while even the NATO States themselves (apart from Belgium), in front of the ICJ, did not rely on the concept of humanitarian intervention.[207]

One may argue that the approval of the relatively new concept of the "Responsibility **192** to Protect" (R2P) implies that humanitarian intervention has by now amounted to international custom, or is currently in the process of doing so. Still, even under the concept of R2P it is mainly, if not exclusively, the UN Security Council that might provide for an authorization to use military force.[208]

---

[200] UN DOC S/RES/1373, 28 September 2001, para. 2(b).

[201] ICJ, *Armed Activities on the Territory of the Congo (DRC v. Uganda)*, ICJ Rep. 2005, 168, 223, para. 147.

[202] Shaw, *International Law*, 7th ed., 2014, 824 *et seq.*; also see UN DOC S/RES/1701, 11 August 2006 referring to the attacks by Hezbollah in Lebanon upon Israel; more restrictive Tams, 20 *EJIL* 2009, 359 (378 *et seq.*).

[203] Lillich, 53 *IowaLRev* 1967, 325 (347); Greenwood, 49 *ICLQ* 2000, 926; *cf.* Simma, 10 *EJIL* 1999, 1; Rodley, in: Weller (ed.), *The Oxford Handbook of the Use of Force in International Law* (2015) 790.

[204] Article 38 (1) (b) ICJ Statute; ICJ, *North Sea Continental Shelf (Germany v. Denmark)*, ICJ Rep. 1969, 3, 43 para. 74; *ICJ, Right of Passage over Indian Territory (Portugal v. India)*, ICJ Rep. 1960, 6, 40.

[205] UN DOC A/RES/2793(XXVI), 7 December 1971; Schachter, 82 *MichLRev* 1984, 1620 (1629).

[206] China (UN DOC S/PV/3988, 24 March 1999); Russia (*ibid.*); India (UN DOC S/1999/328, 26 March 1999); Non-Aligned Movement (UN DOC S/1999/451, 21 April 1999); Rio Group (UN DOC A/53/884, 26 March 1999); Group of 77 (UN DOC A/55/74, 12 May 2000, para. 54).

[207] ICJ, *Legality of Use of Force (Serbia and Montenegro v. Belgium)*, Oral Pleadings of Belgium, CR 99/15, 11, para. 16.

[208] World Summit Outcome, UN DOC A/RES/60/1, 24 October 2005, paras. 79, 139; UN DOC S/RES/1674, 28 April 2006; UN DOC A/59/565, 2 December 2004, para. 203.

193   Yet, if one were to take the position that a humanitarian intervention constitutes a violation of the UN Charter, it still remains a matter of discussion whether, by its character, it would then also constitute a manifest violation thereof, and could thus also amount to a crime of aggression. It was during the 2010 Review Conference, that the then Legal Adviser of the United States Department of State insisted that the inclusion of that sentence had to be understood in a way that any humanitarian intervention carried out, in order to prevent genocide, war crimes, or crimes against humanity, could *ipso facto* not constitute a manifest violation of the UN Charter.[209] A respective understanding to that effect, as proposed by the United States, was however not adopted.[210] Yet, this does not automatically indicate that such humanitarian intervention would then amount to a manifest violation of the UN Charter, in light of its goals and hence its character.[211]

dd) Implicit authorizations by the UN Security Council and the "revitalization" of previous UN Security Council resolutions

194   Chapter VII of the UN Charter enables the UN Security Council to authorize measures which are necessary to maintain peace and security, including the authorization to use military force. In 2003, the United States, as well as the United Kingdom, given the absence of an explicit UN Security Council authorization to use military force against Iraq, tried to justify their invasion of Iraq by relying on an "implicit" authorization contained in UN Security Council Resolution 1441 (2002), and/or on an alleged "revitalization" of the authorization to use all necessary means to restore peace and security in the region as contained in Resolution 678 (1990).[212] Those attempts were however vehemently rejected by the majority of States,[213] although due to the lack of precedence and in light of the somewhat divided scholarly views on the matter, the invasion might not have, at the time, amounted to a manifest violation of the UN Charter.[214]

195   It is in light of these very experiences that the UN Security Council has in its more recent practice either specifically stated that it only authorized measures under Article 41 of the UN Charter (*i. e.* non-military measures),[215] or that the use of military force would require an additional resolution.[216] At least in those latter cases, the use of military force without such additional explicit authorization would then amount to a manifest violation of the UN Charter, and hence constitute a crime of aggression.

---

[209] Koh/Buchwald, 109 *AJIL* 2015, 257 (273).

[210] Mancini, 81 *NordJIL*2012, 227 (236).

[211] McDougall, *The Crime of Aggression under the Rome Statute of the International Criminal Court,* 2013, 162; also see *supra* mns. 233 *et seq.*

[212] UN DOC S/2003/350, 21 March 2003; UN DOC S/2003/351, 21 March 2003; Foreign & Commonwealth Office UK, *Iraq: Legal Position Concerning the Use of Force,* 17 March 2003, https://www.publications.parliament.uk/pa/cm200203/cmselect/cmfaff/405/3030407.htm (last accessed May 2019).

[213] Russia, France, China and Chile (UN DOC S/PV.4714, 7 March 2003); the Non-Aligned Movement and the League of Arab States (UN DOC S/PV.4726, 26 March 2003); Belgium (UN DOC A/58/PV.8, 23 September 2003); Germany (Federal Administrative Court/Bundesverwaltungsgericht, Judgment of 21 June 2005, 2 WD 12.04).

[214] Ambos, *Treatise on International Criminal Law, Volume II,* 2014, 201.

[215] See the practice relating to sanctions on Iran: UN DOCs S/RES/1737, 23 December 2006; S/RES/1747, 24 March 2007; S/R S/1803, 3 March 2008; S/RES/1929, 9 June 2010.

[216] See already UN DOC S/RES/1737, 23 December 2006, para. 24 c), which "[adopt further appropriate measures under Article 41 of Chapter VII of the Charter of the United Nations to persuade Iran to comply with these resolutions and the requirements of the IAEA, and] underlines that further decisions will be required should such additional measures be necessary", thereby not even referring to measures according to Article 42 but only to Article 41 of the Charter of the United Nations; the same provision has been repeated verbatim in the following resolutions.

ee) Intervention upon invitation

Another contentious scenario which might, depending upon the circumstances of the **196** individual case, amount to a manifest violation of the UN Charter as contemplated in Article 8 *bis*, relates to "interventions upon invitation", *i.e.* military interventions by foreign troops in an internal armed conflict upon the invitation of the legitimate government of the State concerned.[217] Given a valid (rather than a fabricated) official invitation by the government of the territorial State concerned, that State's sovereignty is considered not to be violated by following up on the invitation, hence neither amounting to an illegal use of force, nor even less an act of aggression, as defined in Article 8 *bis*. This view is supported, *inter alia*, by recent State practice including the sending of a Regional Assistance Mission to the Solomon Islands (created by the Pacific Islands Forum in order to restore international security)[218], as well as the French intervention in Mali since 2012.

However, in situations when the respective government is no longer to be considered **197** the effective government of the State concerned (and thus no longer able to represent the State or to issue a legally valid "invitation" or consent), intervention to support such government becomes illegal.[219] Yet, depending on the facts of the ground, which in many cases will be disputed, such use of force might not yet be "manifestly" illegal, as required by Article 8 *bis* so as to constitute a crime of aggression.

On the other hand, where the intervening State uses a fabricated "invitation" forced **198** upon the respective government, any such military intervention would then constitute an obvious and manifest violation of the UN Charter.[220]

ff) Rescue of nationals abroad

While in the 19th century, it has been a common practice to use military force in **199** order to protect nationals abroad, the adoption of the UN Charter rendered such actions more controversial, since attacks on individuals abroad do not amount to an armed attack against the home State of the persons concerned itself.[221] Still, there is relevant State practice and *opinio juris*, which indicates that at least a significant number of States take the position that military operations limited in their scale, duration and purpose are legal under international law. Most prominently, following the Israeli rescue operation in the Entebbe incident, the debates in the UN Security Council were inconclusive and the opinion of States on the matter were divided, even when the then UN Secretary General, Kurt Waldheim, condemned these actions as constituting a serious violation of Uganda's sovereignty.[222] The position taken in 1993 by the United Kingdom Foreign and Commonwealth Office might be taken as a guideline in that respect. The United Kingdom argued that "[f]orce may be used [...] against threat to one's nationals if: (a) there is good evidence that the target attacked would otherwise continue to be used by the other State in support of terrorist attacks against one's nationals; (b) there is, effectively, no other way to forestall imminent further attacks on one's nationals; (c) the force employed is proportionate to the threat".[223]

---

[217] Nolte, "Intervention by Invitation", in: *MPEPIL*, mn. 1.

[218] French, 24 *AfricanYbIL* 2005, 337 (426 *et seq.*).

[219] Shaw, *International Law,* 7th ed., 2014, 835; Nolte, "Intervention by Invitation", in: *MPEPIL*, mns. 17 *et seq.*

[220] As to the necessary degree of consent and further details see Nolte, "Intervention by Invitation", in: *MPEPIL*, mn. 16.

[221] Shaw, *International Law,* 7th ed., 2014, 829; Beyerlin, *ZaöRV* 1977, 213 (220).

[222] Shaw, *International Law,* 7th ed., 2014, 829; *cf.* UN DOC S/PV.1939, 9 July 1976, para. 13.

[223] 64 *BYbIL* 1993, 732.

200   On the other hand, and somewhat similar to interventions upon invitation, the concept of using military force in order to (allegedly) rescue threatened nationals may give rise to abuse, the invasion of Grenada in 1983 and of Panama in 1989 by the United States possibly being examples at hand.[224] It would thus, once again, depend on the circumstances of the specific case to determine whether indeed, the operation was not only limited in kind, but also aiming at rescuing nationals genuinely in danger, or whether instead the concept was only relied on to justify an otherwise manifest violation of the UN Charter.

3. Difference between an act and a crime of aggression

> *"For the purpose of this Statute, "crime of aggression" means the planning, preparation, initiation or execution, by a person in a position effectively to exercise control over or to direct the political or military action of a State, of an act of aggression which, by its character, gravity and scale, constitutes a manifest violation of the Charter of the United Nations."*

201   Article 8 *bis* (1) covers the definition of the "crime" of aggression, while (2) (as explained above) covers the definition of the "act" aggression. As noted, an act of aggression will have had to be committed before the crime of aggression can be investigated and prosecuted by the ICC.

202   The introductory words of Article 8 *bis* (1), "[f]or the purpose of this Statute" are identical to the very same formula used in Articles 6, 7 and 8 (2) respectively. The phrase confirms, in line with Article 10,[225] that the definition of the crime of aggression, just like the definition of genocide under Article 6, of crimes against humanity under Article 7, or finally of war crimes under Article 8, is meant to be only relevant for the purpose of the Court's exercise of jurisdiction.

203   The drafters of the Kampala amendment found it appropriate and necessary, however, to further confirm this as part of the enabling Resolution RC/Res.6, which in its Annex III contains "Understandings regarding the amendments to the Rome Statute of the International Criminal Court on the crime of aggression". Understanding no. 4 accordingly provides that:

> *"It is understood that the amendments that address the definition of the act of aggression and the crime of aggression do so for the purpose of this Statute only. The amendments shall, in accordance with article 10 of the Rome Statute, not be interpreted as limiting or prejudicing in any way existing or developing rules of international law for purposes other than this Statute."*

204   This does not prejudice, as indeed Article 10 confirms, that the definition of the crime of aggression, when compared with Articles 6–8, is even more closely interrelated with customary international law generally, and the UN Charter in particular, than those other provisions. It might thus influence the further development of general international law beyond the parameters of international criminal law, the saving clause in the chapeau of Article 8 *bis* (1) notwithstanding.

a) "Crime" of aggression

205   Article 8 *bis* is centred around the term of the "crime of aggression" instead of referring to a "war of aggression", the latter terminology having been used in both, the

---

[224] Shaw, *International Law*, 7th ed., 2014, 830, also see there for further practice.

[225] See generally on Article 10, Triffterer/Heinze, in: Triffterer/Ambos (eds.), *The Rome Statute of the International Criminal Court*, 3rd ed., 2016, Art. 10, in particular mn. 2.

statutes of the two post-World War II International Military Tribunals,[226] as well as in Article 5 of UN General Assembly Resolution 3314. Indeed, while the latter distinguished between "aggression" as such (giving rise to international responsibility only)[227] and a "war of aggression" (only the latter amounting to a "crime against international peace" under the terms of the aforesaid resolution)[228], Article 8 *bis* instead chooses another approach by using the terms "act of aggression" as defined in para. 2 (committed by a State) and the "crime of aggression" as defined in para. 1 (committed by an individual). Article 8 *bis* thus avoids any reference to the loaded notion of a "war of aggression".

Article 8 *bis* (1) provides that certain "acts of aggression", namely those which due to **206** their character, gravity and scale, constitute manifest violations of the UN Charter, entail individual criminal responsibility under the Court's statute. Article 8 *bis* thereby confirms the idea that certain qualified violations of the prohibition of the use of force and thus the *jus ad bellum*, just like serious violations of the *jus in bello*, as well as acts of genocide and crimes against humanity, do not only entail State responsibility, but also carry with them individual criminal sanctions under international law.

This approach, at least as a matter of principle, stands in line with both, Article 6(a) **207** of the Statute of the International Military Tribunal and with Article 5(a) of the Charter of the International Military Tribunal for the Far East, under which the "planning, preparation, initiation or waging of a war of aggression, or a war in violation of international treaties, agreements or assurances" (respectively "the planning, preparation, initiation or waging of a declared or undeclared war of aggression, or a war in violation of international law, treaties, agreements or assurances") constituted a crime against peace. This approach had then been followed in Article 5 (2) of UN General Assembly Resolution 3314 according to which a "war of aggression" was said to constitute a crime against international peace. Finally, it had been the ILC which incorporated the crime of aggression in its 1996 *Draft Code of Crimes against the Peace and Security of Mankind.*[229]

The concept of individual criminal responsibility for the crime of aggression is also **208** mirrored in State practice, since a significant, although not yet overwhelming number of States have, albeit with variations, incorporated the crime of aggression into their respective domestic law or are in the process of doing so.[230] What is more is that recent domestic court decisions[231] have also confirmed the customary law character of the individual criminal responsibility for the crime of aggression arising under international law.

aa) Planning, preparation, initiation or execution

The phrase "planning, preparation, initiation or execution" is, mainly for obvious **209** historical reasons, largely identical to the formula used in both, Article 6(a) of the Charter of the International Military Tribunal in Nuremberg and in Article 5(a) of the Charter of the International Military Tribunal for the Far East, except that in the

---

[226] Article 6 (a) of the Charter of the International Military Tribunal, 1 *Trials of War Criminals before the Nuernberg Military Tribunals under Control Council Law No. 10* 1950, xi; Article 5 (a) of the Charter of the International Military Tribunal for the Far East, in: Boister and Cryer (eds.), *Documents on the Tokyo International Military Tribunal, Charter, Indictment and Judgments,* 2008, 8.

[227] See Article 5 (2), 2nd sentence of GA Resolution 3314 ("Definition of Aggression").

[228] See Article 5 (2), 1st sentence of GA Resolution 3314 ("Definition of Aggression").

[229] International Law Commission, *ILC Yearbook* 1996, ii (part ii), 15, 42.

[230] As to the current status of States having incorporated the crime of aggression into their domestic law, see https://crimeofaggression.info/the-role-of-states/status-of-ratification-and-implementation/[last accessed May 2019].

[231] See *e.g.* the decision of the *House of Lords, R v. Jones et al.,* 45 *ILM* 2006, 992.

English version of Article 8 *bis* (1), the term "waging of a war" was replaced by the term "execution", which is due to the fact that the term "war of aggression" was replaced by the term "act of aggression". This seems to constitute, however, a mere linguistic change rather than a change entailing a difference in substance, even more so since the French version had retained the term "l'exécution d'un acte d'agression". In the equally authentic French versions of the two texts there are however further differences when one compares the Nuremberg and Tokyo formula with the current wording. More specifically, the phrase "la direction, la préparation, le déclenchement ou la poursuite" (of a war of aggression) was replaced by the "planification, la préparation, le lancement ou l'exécution" of an act of aggression. These changes were not all strictly necessitated by the above-mentioned change in terminology of a "war of aggression" (as used in both, the Nuremberg and the Tokyo statutes) versus the "act of aggression" terminology, as used in the Kampala amendment to the Rome Statute.

210   Any proposition that the first three forms of conduct, as contained in Article 8 *bis*, namely the planning, preparation or initiation of an act of aggression are identical as far as their substance is concerned, would make the three terms largely redundant. They thus have to be understood as comprising different, albeit similar, forms of committing the crime of aggression as defined in Article 8 *bis* (1). Accordingly, the mere participation in a single one of the four alternative stages of committing the crime already entails criminal responsibility, provided however that the act of aggression has eventually been committed in the first place.[232]

211   At first glance, the use of the term "planning" ("la planification" in French) might imply that even the mere preparation of plans for a future act of aggression, provided such act of aggression were to reach the threshold provided for in Article 8 *bis* (1), could already amount to the commission of the crime of aggression, even if the aggression as such were then not to take place. Such a far-reaching understanding of the notion of "planning" would have been in line with the fact that under Article 2 (4) of the UN Charter already the threat of the use of force does amount to a violation of international law generally, and the UN Charter in particular.[233] Yet, the third of the Elements of Crimes concerning Article 8 *bis*, adopted simultaneously during the 2010 Review Conference with the amendment proper, confirms that the respective act of aggression must indeed have been committed. It specifically provides:

> *"The act of aggression – the use of armed force by a State against the sovereignty, territorial integrity or political independence of another State, or in any other manner inconsistent with the Charter of the United Nations – was committed."*[234]

212   Accordingly, the act of aggression must have actually taken place so as to render the planning thereof a crime under international law entailing individual criminal responsibility. This deliberate limitation to exclude mere attempts of aggression from the scope of application of Article 8 *bis*, which must be taken at face value, stands in line with customary international law, given that all relevant precedents only considered acts of aggression that had actually taken place to eventually constitute a crime of aggression.[235] Article 25 (3)(f), providing for criminal responsibility in case

---

[232] See mn. 212 as to the requirement that the act of aggression has indeed taken place.

[233] Randelzhofer and Dörr, in: Simma *et al.* (eds.), *The Charter of the United Nations: A Commentary*, 3rd ed., 2012, Art. 2 (4), mn. 42 *et seq.*; Stürchler, *The Threat of Force in International Law*, 2009.

[234] See RC/Res.6, Annex II, *Amendments to the Elements of Crimes for Article 8 bis*, Elements, para. 3, which reads: "The act of aggression – the use of armed force by a State against the sovereignty, territorial integrity or political independence of another State, or in any other manner inconsistent with the Charter of the United Nations – was committed".

[235] ICC–ASP/4/32, Annex II.B, 380.

of attempt, does not contradict this requirement that the actual act of aggression must have taken place since the term "attempt", as used in Article 25 (3)(f), applies to the individual act of participation in a given crime (of aggression as it were) rather than to the act of aggression committed by a State, which act has to be completed.[236] A 2005 SWGCA discussion paper mentioned two (albeit one might say rather academic) examples of such attempts to commit the crime of aggression: first, when a high-level State official begins to participate in a meeting aimed at preparing an act of aggression, before being prevented from taking part in the actual decision-making; and second, when a high-ranking military officer is close to giving an important order in the course of the execution of the use of force, but is prevented from completing the act of ordering.[237]

In line with an interpretation of Article 8 *bis* in conformity with customary interna-   213
tional law, the term "planning" does not cover the general consideration of political plans to eventually, at a later stage only, commit an act of aggression. Rather, it is only the participation in the development of specific (military or other) plans and operations of the State concerned with the commitment of a specific act of aggression that ought to fall within the meaning of the term "planning", in order not to excessively extend the scope of application *ratione temporis* of the crime.

Such a narrow interpretation is confirmed by the French (but also the Spanish) text   214
of Article 8 *bis* (1), which, unlike the Nuremberg and Tokyo precedents, does not use the term "direction" anymore. Yet, this term would have already excluded any such temporal extension, while the French term "planification" (and "planifica" in the Spanish text), as now used in the context of Article 8 *bis*, even more strongly confirms that the notion of "planning" solely refers to the ability of the perpetrator to direct the aggression by way of drawing up "a design or scheme"[238] for the aggression that is then being committed.

This limited understanding of the notion of "planning" is further confirmed by the   215
context of Article 8 *bis* in that the group of possible offenders is defined as those persons able "to exercise control over or to direct the political or military action of a State". This limitation of the scope *ratione personae* of the crime underlines that it is only concrete and specific actions constituting (qualified) violations of the prohibition of the use of force (rather than mere threats of force) that are being criminalized, but not acts which do not yet amount to such violations.

Similar considerations do apply, *mutatis mutandis*, to the notion of "preparation":   216
only those offenders that fulfil the leadership criteria laid down in Article 8 *bis* and then participate (within the meaning of Article 25 of the Rome Statute) in an act of aggression, be it only in its very initial stages, *i. e.* when the aggression is still only being prepared, but not yet implemented, commit the crime of aggression, provided the further criteria of Article 8 *bis* are also fulfilled.

In contrast to the "planning" of an act of aggression, the "preparation" of such an act   217
refers to the taking of concrete steps to implement the plan.[239] *Inter alia*, such preparation may consist, depending on which specific alternative of Article 8 *bis* (2) is being committed by the State concerned (*e. g.* in the transport of weaponry or other military material to be used for the act of aggression, in the actual deployment of troops to the vicinity of a border to start hostilities, or in acts of a similar nature that will, when

---

[236] Mancini, 81 *NordJIL* 2012, 227 (242).
[237] ICC-ASP/2/10, Annex II, as summarized in: Barriga and Kreß (eds.), *The Travaux Préparatoires of the Crime of Aggression*, 2012, 471, 480.
[238] Greenspan, *The Modern Law of Land Warfare*, 1959, 455.
[239] *Ibid.*

seen from an outside perspective, form part and parcel of the forthcoming actual violation of the prohibition of the use of force).

218   In that regard, one has to particularly take note of the decision of the ICJ in the *Nicaragua* case, according to which "in international law there are no rules, other than such rules as may be accepted by the State concerned, by treaty or otherwise, whereby the level of armaments of a sovereign State can be limited".[240] Hence, the participation by a person exercising control of a State in the military build-up of a given State is, in and of itself, legal under international law, and may thus *a fortiori* neither be considered to entail individual criminal responsibility under the heading of "preparation" of the crime of aggression even if, later on, an act of aggression is being committed by that very State.

219   The "initiation" of an act of aggression describes the very commencement of the use of armed force, as defined in Article 8 *bis* (2). Given that various of the alternative acts of aggression as defined in Article 8 *bis* (2) (such as a naval blockade[241] or the mere extension of the presence of armed forces in foreign territory beyond the termination of a stationing agreement[242]) do not require the actual start of hostilities,[243] the question when exactly the respective "act of aggression" is being initiated depends on which form of such an act of aggression is being considered.

220   Finally, the term "execution" covers all subsequent acts of actually carrying out and performing acts of aggression, following the initiation of such acts, as described above.[244]

bb) Persons carrying out the crime of aggression

221   The crime of aggression can be committed only by leaders of the State, to which the underlying act of aggression is attributable. Without this limiting criterion, every individual soldier of the armed forces having contributed to the hostilities would otherwise, as a matter of principle, have to face trial. Article 8 *bis* thus constitutes the only one of the four crimes, for which the Court has substance-matter jurisdiction under Article 5 of the Rome Statute, which limits the range of potential perpetrators of such a crime. This pays tribute to the different nature of the crime of aggression, which, in contrast to the Statute's other crimes listed in Article 5, is not focused on the protection of individuals or on the protection of a given protected group, but rather on the protection of a State from the use of armed force by another State[245] and thereby by the same token also aims at the protection of the international legal system with the prohibition of the use of force at its core.

222   Already Article II (2)(f) of Law No. 10 of 20 December 1945 by the Control Council for Germany[246] considered a "high political, civil or military (including General Staff) position [...] or [a] high position in the financial, industrial or economic life" a prerequisite in order to fall within the group of possible offenders when it comes to crimes against peace. In the same vein in 1950, the ILC concluded that only "high-ranking military personnel and high State officials" could be capable of waging a war of aggression.[247] Accordingly, the consent that also for purposes of the Court's Statute, the

---

[240] ICJ, *Military and Paramilitary Activities in and against Nicaragua (Nicaragua v. United States of America)*, Judgement (Merits), ICJ Rep. 1986, 14, 135, para. 269.

[241] See mn. 148 *et seq.*

[242] See mn. 157 *et seq.*

[243] But see Dinstein, *War, Aggression and Self-Defence*, 5th ed., 2011, 141.

[244] See mn. 219.

[245] Heinsch, 2 *GoJIL* 2010, 713 (722); also see Dinstein, 24 *IsYbHumRts.* 1994, 1 (4 *et seq.*).

[246] Control Council Law No. 10, 1 *Trials of War Criminals before the Nuernberg Military Tribunals under Control Council Law No. 10*, 1950, xvi.

[247] International Law Commission, Principles of International Law recognized in the Charter of the Nuernberg Tribunal and in the Judgment of the Tribunal, with commentaries, *ILC Yearbook* 1950, ii, 376, para. 117.

crime of aggression ought to remain a leadership crime became established early in the drafting process for what is now Article 8 *bis*, namely in the 2002 Coordinator's Paper of the Preparatory Committee's Ninth Session.[248]

The use of the term "by a person" in Article 8 *bis* (1) exercising control over or **223** directing the political or military action of a State does not indicate that only one person can be responsible of the crime of aggression. As a matter of fact, footnote 1 attached to the second Element of Crimes adopted concerning the crime of aggression and related to the leadership requirement confirms in unequivocal terms that "[w]ith respect to an act of aggression, more than one person may be in a position that meets these criteria of exercising such degree of control".[249] This stands in line with the judgment of the United States Military Tribunal which, in the *High Command* case, stressed that even in a dictatorship, more than one individual can bear responsibility for the planning, preparation, initiation or the execution of an act of aggression.[250]

In practice, the group of people exercising sufficient control over or directing the **224** political or military action of a State, in order to be covered by the leadership requirement as set out in Article 8 *bis* (1), encompasses at the very least heads of States and governments, as well as ministers of defence and other military leaders such as high-level generals.[251] Given the wording of the provision which refers to the ability to effectively exercise or direct the action of the State from which the act of aggression emanates, it is the factual capability to exercise such control or direction that is decisive, rather than the formal rank, *de jure* position or title of the person concerned.[252] Accordingly, also mere *de facto* heads of States or government or *de facto* commanders of armed forces of a State, who are in a position of effective control of their respective State, are subject to the Court's aggression-related substance-matter jurisdiction.

At the same time, heads of State exercising merely ceremonial functions, but not **225** being able, neither *de jure* nor *de facto*, to participate in the decision-making process which leads to the alleged act of aggression contemplated in Article 8 *bis* (2), are not capable of committing the crime of aggression within the meaning of the Court's Statute.

In order to possibly commit the crime of aggression, a person concerned must either **226** have been able to exercise control over or alternatively been able to direct the political or military action of the State in question. While the "to direct" limb of the phrase hints more at a positive action taken by the person concerned, the "to control" limb seems to indicate that the crime of aggression might also be committed by way of supervision,

---

[248] UN DOC PCNICC/2002/WGCA/RT.1, in: Barriga and Kreß (eds.), *The Travaux Préparatoires of the Crime of Aggression,* 2012, 398: "For the purpose of this Statute, a crime of aggression means an act committed by a person who, being in a position to exercise control over or direct the political or military action of a State [...]." In the Coordinator's paper of the tenth session of the Preparatory Committee, the word "effectively" has been added to the definition, UN DOC PCNICC/2002/WGCA/RT.1/Rev.1, in: Barriga and Kreß (eds.), *The Travaux Préparatoires of the Crime of Aggression,* 2012, 412: "[...] being in a position effectively to exercise control over or to direct the political or military action of a State [...]".

[249] RC/Res.6, Annex II, *Amendments to the Elements of Crimes for Article 8 bis,* Elements, para. 2, fn. 1, emphasis added.

[250] *High Command case (United States of America v. Wilhelm von Leeb et al.),* 12 *Trials of War Criminals Before the Nuernberg Military Tribunals Under Control Council Law No. 10* 1950, 462, 486: "No matter how absolute his authority, Hitler alone could not formulate a policy of aggressive war and alone implement that policy by preparing, planning and waging such a war".

[251] Heinsch, 2 *GoJIL* 2010, 713 (722).

[252] UN DOC PCNICC/2002/WGCA/L.1/Add.1, 18 January 2002, Preparatory Commission for the International Criminal Court, Historical Review of Developments relating to Aggression, Addendum, 32, referring to the Nuremberg trials; Werle and Jessberger, *Principles of International Criminal Law,* 3rd ed., 2014, 542.

provided the person concerned could thereby exercise effective influence on the course of action leading to the act of aggression.

227   Within the framework of the SWGCA, it was considerably debated whether industrialists who are closely involved with the State's actions should be covered by this provision. The post-1945 Nuremberg trials against high-ranking German industrialists demonstrated the potential of industrialists' involvement in the crime of aggression. As a matter of fact, Article II (2)(f) of Control Council Law No. 10 of 1945 included persons as possible indictees of crimes against peace, who "held high position in the financial, industrial or economic life" of Germany, one of its Allies, co-belligerents or satellites. In the trial of the major war criminals, Gustav Krupp, the head of the Krupp AG, was indicted, *inter alia*, for participation in the Nazi conspiracy to commit crimes against peace and its eventual commission.[253] The final judgment stressed that business men cooperated in Hitler's aggressive war and made themselves parties to his plan[254]. Though in the subsequent *I.G. Farben* and *Krupp* cases, all defendants were acquitted of charges with regard to crimes against peace due to a lack of evidence, the respective tribunals stated that this should not be interpreted as excluding such responsibility in general.[255] In the *High Command* and in the *Ministries* cases, the tribunals adopted a "shape or influence" criterion, relying on whether the defendants had had the power to shape or influence the State's policy.[256] In the *Roechling* case, the leader of the coal and metal business Roechling was convicted of having encouraged and contributed to the preparation and conduct of aggressive wars.[257]

228   However, a SWGCA proposal to use language closer to that of the Nuremberg decisions, namely the "shape and influence" formula instead of the "exercise control over or to direct" formula, was rejected, which might be perceived as a legitimate decision, given that in democracies the "shape and influence" criterion might affect an excessively large range of individuals.[258] On the other side, the actual terms of Article 8 *bis* (1) do not *per se* exclude economic (or religious, or revolutionary) leaders from criminal responsibility, as long as their position allows them to exercise control over or to direct a State's political or military action.[259]

229   It is further sufficient that any possible indictee has exercised control over or directed either the political *or* the military action of the State concerned. In the former case, *i. e.* in the case of a political direction or control, there must however be a link between such

---

[253] Before being considered medically unfit for trial, 1 *Trial of the Major War Criminals before the International Military Tribunal* 1947, 27 42, 75.

[254] Judgment, 22 *Trial of the Major War Criminals before the International Military Tribunal* 1948, 424 *et seq.*, 468.

[255] *Farben case (United States of America v. Krauch et al.)*, 8 *Trials of War Criminals before the Nuernberg Military Tribunals under Control Council Law No. 10*, 1952, 1081, 1125 *et seq.*; *Krupp case (United States of America v. Krupp et al.)*, 9 *Trials of War Criminals before the Nuernberg Military Tribunals under Control Council Law No. 10*, 1950, 390, 393; also see Heller, 18 *EJIL* 2007, 477 (483 *et seq.*).

[256] *High Command case (United States of America v. Wilhelm von Leeb et al.)*, 12 *Trials of War Criminals Before the Nuernberg Military Tribunals Under Control Council Law No. 10*, 1950, 462, 489; *Ministries case (United States v. von Weizsäcker et al.)*, 14 *Trials of War Criminals Before the Nuernberg Military Tribunals Under Control Council Law No. 10*, 1952, 314, 425.

[257] *Roechling case (Military Government of the French Zone of Occupation in Germany v. Roechling et al.)*, 14 *Trials of War Criminals before the Nuernberg Military Tribunals under Control Council Law No. 10*, 1952, 1075, 1095. Later on, the conviction was reversed by the *Superior Military Government Court of the French Zone of Occupation in Germany*.

[258] Ambos, 53 *GYbIL* 2010, 463 (490).

[259] Ambos, 53 *GYbIL* 2010, 463 (490); Heinsch, 2 *GoJIL* 2010, 713 (723); Sayapin, *The Crime of Aggression in International Criminal Law*, 2014, 260; Werle and Jessberger, *Principles of International Criminal Law*, 3rd ed., 2014, 550.

a political role on the one hand, and the military action giving rise to the indictment relating to the crime of aggression on the other.

Finally, the term "political or military action" ought to be understood in light of the **230** overall object and purpose of the provision. Accordingly, it is only the control or direction of "political or military action" that leads to an act of aggression that is relevant in order to determine whether a person can have possibly committed the crime of aggression.

Only persons that direct the actions of a State are suitable offenders under Article 8 **231** *bis* (1). Article 8 *bis* (1) thus reiterates the inter-state character of the crime of aggression, as laid down in the chapeau of Article 8 *bis* (2) with its double statehood requirement ("by a State"/"against […] another State").[260]

Since the text of Article 8 *bis* (1) refers to "a" State (rather than to "his or her State"), **232** there is no requirement that the offender possesses the nationality of the State from which the underlying act of aggression would then emanate. As a matter of fact, there have been situations in the past where a ruler of State A (also) controlled the political or military action of State B, leading State B to then commit an act of aggression.

b) "Act" of aggression as a manifest violation of the UN Charter

In order to eventually constitute a crime of aggression, the underlying act of **233** aggression must, first and foremost, constitute a violation of the UN Charter. According to Article 2 (4) of the UN Charter,[261] all UN Members shall refrain in their international relations from the threat or use of force against the territorial integrity or political independence of any state, or in any other manner inconsistent with the purposes of the UN. The Charter itself knows two exceptions to this provision, namely either an authorization by the UN Security Council to use force under Chapter VII (possibly combined with Chapter VIII in case of military action by a regional organization or arrangement) or the right of self-defence under Article 51 of the UN Charter (the Charter's enemy State clauses in Articles 53 and 107 having become obsolete).[262]

Unlike Article 2 (4) of the UN Charter, which in its last part refers to the use of force **234** "inconsistent with the Purposes of the United Nations",[263] Article 8 *bis* simply refers to (aggravated) uses of force in (manifest) "violation of the Charter". It is however generally acknowledged that for purposes of the Charter prohibition of the use of force, such acts are lawful not only in those cases that are explicitly specified in the Charter itself as exceptions to Article 2 (4), but also in scenarios universally recognized under customary international law as accordingly not amounting to a violation of the UN Charter.[264] Given that Article 8 *bis* (1) in turn refers back to the question as to whether a given use of force constitutes a violation of the UN Charter, exceptions to the prohibition of the use of force, as recognized in customary international law, are also relevant when it comes to making a finding on the crime of aggression as set out in Article 8 *bis*.

---

[260] See mns. 110 *et seq.*

[261] 15 UNCIO 335.

[262] As to the possibility of deleting the enemy State clauses from the Charter as part of an overall reform see UN DOCs A/RES/50/52, 11 December 1995, para. 3; A/RES/60/1, 16 September 2005, para. 177; as well as Eitel, in: Varwick and Zimmermann (eds.), *Die Reform der Vereinten Nationen – Bilanz und Perspektiven*, 2006, 315.

[263] As to this notion see Randelzhofer and Dörr, in: Simma *et al.* (eds.), *The Charter of the United Nations: A Commentary*, 3rd ed., 2012, Art. 2 (4), mns. 37 *et seq.*

[264] Randelzhofer and Dörr, in: Simma *et al.* (eds.), *The Charter of the United Nations: A Commentary*, 3rd ed., 2012, Art. 2 (4), mn. 38.

235   In line with Article 2 (4) of the UN Charter, which is addressed to all members of the organization, Article 8 *bis* (1) refers to violations of the UN Charter (rather than violations of customary law), which as a matter of fundamental rules of treaty law only applies to its contracting parties. In the unlikely (but not completely academic[265]) event that individuals being nationals of a State, which is not a member of the UN, but nevertheless bound by the Kampala amendment on the crime of aggression, are responsible for the use of armed force, the question arises whether such acts may then possibly amount to "violations of the Charter" despite the fact that the State concerned is not bound by the UN Charter as such. Yet, an interpretation of Article 8 *bis* in light of its object and purpose seems to indicate that what is meant by Article 8 *bis* are not (manifest) violations of the UN Charter *per se*, but rather also violations of the substantive parallel customary law prohibition on the use of force[266] as enshrined in the Charter, also being binding upon non-member States by virtue of customary law.

236   As confirmed by no. 2 of the introduction to the Elements of Crimes relevant for Article 8 *bis*, as adopted in the 2010 Review Conference, "[t]here is no requirement to prove that the perpetrator has made a legal evaluation as to whether the use of armed force was inconsistent with the Charter of the United Nations."

237   In contrast to the rather broad definition of aggression, as contained in the UN General Assembly Resolution 3314 for the purposes of State responsibility, and so as to eventually provide guidance to the UN Security Council when making a determination under Article 39 of the UN Charter, which does not require any aggressive intent and, besides contains a broad list of possible acts of aggression[267], Article 8 *bis* limits criminal accountability to severe acts by using a threshold that can be found neither in the UN Charter, nor in Resolution 3314. This threshold clause captures the "qualitative difference" between an act of aggression and the individual crime.[268]

238   This part of Article 8 *bis* (1) has accordingly been criticized for providing a *carte blanche* for all uses of armed force that do not yet amount to a certain scale,[269] thereby eventually leading to a weakening of the general prohibition of the use of force, as contained in Article 2 (4) of the UN Charter and in customary international law, at least when it comes to the use of military force below the threshold now laid down in Article 8 *bis*. On the other hand, a comparison with the regime of international humanitarian law, where during the last 20 years a line of jurisprudence involving only serious violations of international humanitarian law has evolved, indicates that the prosecution of merely such grave violations can nevertheless strengthen the overall obedience towards the general rule (even if not all violations of international humanitarian law were falling within the jurisdiction of the various international criminal courts and tribunals).[270]

---

[265] See *e.g.* the situation of Palestine having become a contracting party of the Rome Statute without being at the same time a member of the United Nations, and possibly also having become bound by the Kampala amendment on the crime of aggression under the principle codified in Article 40 (5) of the Vienna Convention on the Law of treaties, given that Palestine acceded to the Rome Statute after the Kampala amendment had already entered into force; as to the various ways to become bound by the aggression-related amendments see *infra* mns. 299 *et seq.*

[266] As to this questions, *i.e.* the identity in content of the treaty-based prohibition of the use of force and the respective customary law prohibition see *ICJ, Military and Paramilitary Activities in and against Nicaragua (Nicaragua v. United States of America)*, Judgement (Merits), ICJ Rep. 1986, 14, 93 *et seq.*, paras. 174 *et seq.*

[267] See mns. 126 *et seq.*

[268] Ambos, *Treatise on International Criminal Law, Volume II*, 2014, 199.

[269] Heinsch, 2 *GoJIL* 2010, 713 (726); Paulus, 20 *EJIL* 2009, 1117 (1122).

[270] Heinsch, 2 *GoJIL* 2010, 713 (731); also see Öberg, 873 *RevRC* 2009, 163.

3. Difference between an act and a crime of aggression

As the drafting history indicates, the said restriction of manifest violations of the UN **239** Charter was inserted in order "to exclude some borderline cases"[271] of the use of force, which, while amounting to a violation of Article 2 (4) of the UN Charter, did not warrant to be considered a crime of aggression. More specifically, the threshold clause is meant to serve a twofold purpose.

For one, the formula was meant to exclude "minor border skirmishes and other **240** small-scale incidents"[272] from the scope of application of Article 8 *bis*. This was meant to take into account the judgment of the ICJ in the *Nicaragua* case (as confirmed by both the Court itself in the *Oil Platforms* case, and by the Eritrea-Ethiopia Claims Commission). In the former case, the Court had observed for one that it is "necessary to distinguish the most grave forms of the use of force (those constituting an armed attack) from other less grave forms".[273] It also found that in considering whether a given operation amounts to an armed attack, "its scale and effects" have to be taken into account.[274] By the same token, the Court had further found that "a mere frontier incident" does not yet amount to an armed attack,[275] while the Eritrea-Ethiopia Claims Commission even went further when stating that "[l]ocalized border encounters between small infantry units, even those involving the loss of life, do not constitute an armed attack for purposes of the Charter [of the UN]".[276] Accordingly, it was argued that a somewhat more limited use of military force, while prohibited under Article 2 (4) of the UN Charter, should even less constitute a crime of aggression.

At the same time, the restriction was also inserted so as to exclude from its **241** scope of application acts whose illegal character would be debatable rather than manifest.[277]

The need for this restriction was however seriously debated in the SWGCA. In the **242** end, the opponents of any such limitation agreed in return for the removal of other restrictions. It is against this background that the requirement of a "war of aggression" was deleted from former drafts, and that any limitations to the list of potential acts of aggression (as defined in UN General Assembly Resolution 3314) were rejected. Instead, Article 8 *bis* now contains the criterion that any act of aggression within the meaning of Article 8 *bis* (2) must also by its character, gravity and scale constitute a manifest violation of the UN Charter.

This narrow concept was confirmed in Understandings nos. 6 and 7 annexed to RC/ **243** Res. 6 (2010), which provide that:

> "6. *It is understood that aggression is the most serious and dangerous form of the illegal use of force; and that a determination whether an act of aggression has been committed requires consideration of all the circumstances of each particular case,*

---

[271] Informal inter-sessional meeting of the Special Working Group on the Crime of Aggression, Assembly of States Parties, 5th session 2006, ICCASP/5/SWGCA/INF.1, 5 September 2006, para. 19.

[272] Barriga, in: Barriga and Kreß (eds.), *The Travaux Préparatoires of the Crime of Aggression,* 2012, 3 (29).

[273] ICJ, *Military and Paramilitary Activities in and against Nicaragua (Nicaragua v. United States of America),* Judgement (Merits), ICJ Rep. 1986, 14, 101, para. 191; see also ICJ, *Oil Platforms (Iran v. USA),* Judgement, ICJ Rep. 2003, 161, 187, para. 51.

[274] ICJ, *Military and Paramilitary Activities in and against Nicaragua (Nicaragua v. United States of America),* Judgement (Merits), ICJ Rep. 1986, 14, 103, para. 195.

[275] *Ibid.*

[276] *Eritrea-Ethiopia Claims Commission,* Jus ad Bellum (Partial Award, Ethiopia's Claims 1–8, 19 December 2005), 135 *ILR* 2009, 479, para. 11.

[277] Barriga, in: Barriga and Kreß (eds.), *The Travaux Préparatoires of the Crime of Aggression,* 2012, 3 (29).

including the gravity of the acts concerned and their consequences, in accordance with the Charter of the United Nations."

244   respectively:

> *"7. It is understood that in establishing whether an act of aggression constitutes a manifest violation of the Charter of the United Nations, the three components of character, gravity and scale must be sufficient to justify a "manifest" determination. No one component can be significant enough to satisfy the manifest standard by itself."*

245   Understanding no. 6, just like Article 8 *bis* (2) itself, draws largely on language forming part of UN General Assembly Resolution 3314. In line with preambular paragraph 5 of the annex to the said resolution, which contains the definition of aggression, Understanding no. 6 perceives aggression as "the most serious and dangerous form of the illegal use of force", without however thereby adding much (if anything) to the actual definition contained in Article 8 *bis* itself, given that the very text of Article 8 *bis* even requires a manifest violation of international law.

246   Moreover, Understanding no. 6, almost (though not completely *verbatim*) echoing Article 2 of UN General Assembly Resolution 3314, "requires consideration of all the circumstances of each particular case, including the gravity of the acts concerned and their consequences, in accordance with the Charter of the United Nations". While Article 2 of the UN General Assembly Resolution 3314 was meant to acknowledge the prerogatives of the UN Security Council in making (or not making) a determination of aggression, as contemplated in Article 39 of the UN Charter,[278] this part of Understanding no. 6 in turn is addressed to the organs of the Court when making determinations as to whether an act of aggression has been committed. In doing so, the gravity of the acts concerned and their consequences, in accordance with the UN Charter, have to be then taken into account. It is thus somewhat striking that under the Kampala formula, the gravity of the relevant act serves a twofold purpose: under Understanding no. 6 it contributes to determine whether (in line with UN General Assembly Resolution 3314) even an act of aggression has taken place. Once this first threshold is fulfilled, any such act (accordingly thereby amounting to an act of aggression) must then be judged upon once again, *inter alia*, in light of its gravity in order to determine whether it amounts to a manifest violation of the UN Charter and thus constitutes a crime of aggression. It is however difficult to see what different factors could then be taken into account in order to determine the gravity of such an act when it comes to this second layer of gravity. What is more is that Understanding no. 6 refers to the gravity of the relevant act and its consequences, while Article 8 *bis* (1) simply refers to the gravity as such. This seems to imply that for purposes of the second step, *i.e.* the process of determining a manifest violation of the Charter, and thus potentially a crime of aggression, the consequences of the act ought not to be further taken into account. This is due to the fact, that such consequences seem to not *ipso jure* form part of the concept of "gravity", as confirmed by the wording of Understanding no. 6 where, as shown, the notion of "gravity" and the "consequences" of an act are put side by side.

247   Article 8 *bis* (1) mentions three specific criteria to determine whether an act of aggression constitutes a manifest violation of the UN Charter, namely the character,

---

[278] Article 2 of the Definition of Aggression reads: "The first use of armed force by a State in contravention of the Charter shall constitute *prima facie* evidence of an act of aggression although the Security Council may, in conformity with the Charter, conclude that a determination that an act of aggression has been committed would not be justified in the light of other relevant circumstances, including the fact that the acts concerned or their consequences are not of sufficient gravity."

gravity and scale of such an act. Understanding no. 7 then further attempts to clarify the relationship between the three factors of character, gravity and scale.

For one, by referring in the plural to the fact that the three components of character, **248** gravity and scale must be sufficient ("doivent être suffisamment importants" in the French version) to justify a "manifest" determination, it seems to provide that all of those three components must be fulfilled to the degree necessary.[279] On the other hand, the wording of the last sentence of Understanding no. 7, which refers to the fact that "[n]o one component can be significant enough to satisfy the manifest standard by itself" leaves in the blur whether all three components – character, gravity and scale – must be fulfilled,[280]or whether the fulfilment of two of them would be sufficient. During the drafting process of what was to become Understanding no. 7, a consensus on this issue was hard to reach. Notably, in particular the United States, despite of not even being a State party to the Rome Statute and thus not being subject to the Court's jurisdiction under Article 15 *bis* (5),[281] favoured a cumulative approach, thereby argu-ably *per se* excluding humanitarian interventions from the scope of application of Article 8 *bis*, given the alleged humanitarian character of such military operations.[282] Not least the Iranian delegation argued in turn that the fulfilment of two of these three criterions ought to be sufficient; however, the final compromise as proposed by Canada and the United States was adopted without opposition.[283]

The final wording of what is now Understanding no. 7 constitutes a compromise, **249** which, however, does not necessarily solve the issue. On the one hand, the second sentence of Understanding no. 7, and in particular the phrase "[n]o one component […] by itself" could be read as a support for a strict interpretation of the manifest standard, *i. e.* one under which the fulfilment of only two of the three elements would suffice for an act of aggression to amount to a manifest violation of the UN Charter.

On the other hand, an interpretation of Article 8 *bis* (1) as such in line with its very **250** wording, as required by Article 31 (1) of the Vienna Convention on the Law of Treaties, militates in favour of a cumulative requirement, since Article 8 *bis* (1) uses the conjunctive "and" instead of an "or" ("by its character, gravity and scale"). Likewise, the first sentence of Understanding no. 7 refers to "the three components of character, gravity and scale" which "must be sufficient". While this part of Understanding no. 7 is not fully conclusive, given that it could also be read as meaning that apart from those three components there is no need for further criteria to be also fulfilled, it seems that the last sentence of Understanding no. 7 at least requires that two of the components are fulfilled. Such interpretation, *i. e.* that one component is not sufficient, while a fulfilment of all the three of them is not required either, would also be in line with the character of Understanding no. 7 as a compromise formula. Such result can also be understood as being compatible with the very wording of Article 8 *bis* (1) ("character, gravity and scale"), since the "and" contained therein could very well be understood as not necessarily requiring that all three components of "character and gravity and scale" are fulfilled at the same time.

The term "character" refers, as confirmed by the French wording ("par sa nature"), to **251** the nature of the act of aggression to be possibly qualified as a crime of aggression. Given the drafting history of Article 8 *bis* (1), this is to be understood as referring to the

---

[279] Werle and Jessberger, *Principles of International Criminal Law,* 3rd ed., 2014, 549.
[280] Ambos, 53 *GYbIL* 2010, 463 (484).
[281] See *infra* mns. 391 *et seq.*
[282] See mns. 190 *et seq.*
[283] Kreß, Barriga, Grover and von Holtzendorff, in: Barriga and Kreß (eds.), *The Travaux Préparatoires of the Crime of Aggression,* 2012, 81 (96 *et seq.*).

(actual) subjective motivation of the persons responsible for the use of force, *i.e.* whether they rather aim at occupying or annexing foreign territory or whether instead they, for example, aim at protecting fundamental human rights of a given population.[284]

252 The terms "gravity" and "scale" are intertwined and somewhat hard to distinguish. Yet, given that it cannot be assumed that the text contains redundant wording, one might say that the gravity requirement relates more to the seriousness or significance of the use of force, *i.e.* constitutes more of a qualitative criterion, while the scale is more a quantitative criterion. This is confirmed, once again, by the French and Spanish texts of Article 8 *bis* (1), in which the terms "gravité"/"gravedad" versus "ampleur"/"escala" make this distinction clearer. Accordingly, the notion of "gravity" involves a determination as to the nature of the means used. To give but one example, it thus seems easier to assume that the invasion or bombardment of a foreign country, contemplated in Article 8 *bis* (2)(a) and (b) respectively can, by their very nature, more easily fulfil the criterion of gravity, than, for example, a mere violation of a stationing agreement, provided for in Article 8 *bis* (2)(e).

253 In determining the gravity of an act of aggression, the amount of damage caused to the attacked State ought to also be taken into account. However, in this regard, it has to be noted that for purposes of Article 8 *bis* it is irrelevant whether such damages by the same token did (or did not) amount to a violation of applicable rules of *jus in bello* (and possibly even war crimes within the meaning of Article 8). This is due to the fundamental distinction of *jus ad bellum* and *jus in bello*, only the former being regulated by Article 8 *bis*.

254 As previously mentioned[285], the notion of "scale" ("ampleur" in French/"escala" in Spanish) refers to the level or magnitude of the alleged act of aggression. In order to evaluate such "scale", one has to take into account the use of armed force *ratione loci* and *ratione temporis*. Put otherwise, the more widespread and the longer such force is being employed, the easier it is to make a positive finding as to the required scale of the military operation, so as to constitute a crime of aggression.

255 It is worth noting, however, that only those parts of the military operation that, by the same token, run counter to the prohibition of the use of force might be taken into account. Thus, for example, a military use of force justified under Article 51 of the UN Charter might constitute an illegal use of force to the extent to which the alleged acts of self-defence are no longer proportionate, *e.g.* because they extend far beyond the actual armed confrontation and threat.[286] In the same vein, what might constitute, like in the case of the attack of the United States against Iraq in 2003, an act of aggression, can later turn into an occupation in line with international law, once the UN Security Council, acting under Chapter VII of the Charter, provides for a legal basis for such an occupation.[287]

256 According to the amendments to the Elements of Crimes relating to Article 8 *bis* adopted in the 2010 Review Conference, "[t]he term 'manifest' is an objective qualification",[288] which is thus independent from subjective opinions[289] as to the legality or illegality of the respective military operation or, indeed, as to its character as a manifest violation of the UN Charter. As a matter of course, as again the Elements of Crimes

---

[284] See also mns. 190 *et seq.*

[285] See mn. 252.

[286] See *e.g.* the example of the taking of an airport several hundred kilometers away from the actual front given by the *ICJ, Armed Activities on the Territory of the Congo (DRC v. Uganda)*, ICJ Rep. 2005, 168, 223, para. 147.

[287] UN DOC S/RES/1483, 22 May 2003.

[288] RC/Res.6, Annex II, Amendments to the Elements of Crimes for Article 8 *bis*, Introduction, para. 3.

[289] Heinsch, 2 *GoJIL* 2010, 713 (727).

relating to Article 8 *bis* confirm, there is neither a "requirement to prove that the perpetrator has made a legal evaluation as to the 'manifest' nature of the violation of the Charter of the United Nations".[290] The perpetrator must have been aware, however, as again confirmed by the Elements of Crimes relating to Article 8 *bis*, "of the factual circumstances that established that such a use of armed force was inconsistent with the Charter of the United Nations", and, besides, he must have also been aware of the further "factual circumstances that established such a manifest violation of the Charter of the United Nations".[291]

The very same considerations would then accordingly also apply *mutatis mutandis* to   **257** the various components constituting the manifest character of the violation of the UN Charter, namely the factual elements determining the character, the gravity, and the scale of the act of aggression.

In practice, the Court might have difficulties assessing whether a given act of   **258** aggression constitutes a manifest violation of the UN Charter. As a court of international criminal law, some consider its legitimacy to rule on questions of *jus ad bellum* as doubtful[292], especially concerning "grey area" cases. An excessive use of its respective authority might provide States with a further reason to criticize the Court.[293] On the other hand, the long and tedious process of including the crime of aggression into the Rome Statute indicates that, eventually, the States parties must have been very aware of the responsibility and competence they were thereby referring to the ICC.

At the same time, the requirement of a "manifest" violation might lead to a situation   **259** in which in almost all relevant cases justifications for an illegal use of force might be adduced that are, while being wrong on substance, not that far-fetched so as to enable the State concerned, as well as the alleged offenders, to at least make a plausible claim that the said use of force was not "manifestly" illegal.[294] This involves the risk of making Article 8 *bis de facto* not only jurisdiction-wise (given the Court's limited scope of jurisdiction under Article 15 *bis*),[295] but also substance-wise, largely a *lettre morte* or, at best, symbolic in nature.

The broad notion of "manifest" violations of the prohibition of the use of force, and   **260** the ensuing "grey areas" when it comes to contentious cases of the use of force, has to be also seen in light of the principle of *nullum crimen, nulla poena sine lege certa* and in light of Article 22 (2) of the Rome Statute, which provides that "[t]he definition of a crime shall be strictly construed [...] shall not be extended by analogy", and that "[i]n case of ambiguity, the definition shall be interpreted in favour of the person being investigated, prosecuted or convicted".[296] That provision will prove its particular relevance with regard to criminal responsibility arising from the above-mentioned grey areas of the use of force. In such instances, the Court will then have to take into account not only the case law of the ICJ, but also relevant State practice (as well as the practice

---

[290] See RC/Res.6, Annex II, *Amendments to the Elements of Crimes for Article 8 bis*, Elements, Introduction, para. 4.

[291] RC/Res.6, Annex II, *Amendments to the Elements of Crimes for Article 8 bis*, Elements, paras. 4, 6; see also further Pigaroff and Robinson, in: Triffterer/Ambos (eds.), *The Rome Statute of the International Criminal Court*, 3rd ed., 2016, Art. 30, *passim*.

[292] McDougall, *The Crime of Aggression under the Rome Statute of the International Criminal Court*, 2013, 158; Fife, in: Bergsmo (ed.), *Human Rights and Criminal Justice for the Downtrodden: Essays in Honour of Asbjorn Eide*, 2003, 53 (73); Kreß, 20 *Leiden JIL* 2007, 851 (859).

[293] McDougall, *The Crime of Aggression under the Rome Statute of the International Criminal Court*, 2013, 163.

[294] See for such proposition Paulus, 20 *EJIL* 2009, 1117 (1122 *et seq.*).

[295] For details *infra* mns. 273 *et seq.*

[296] For details as to Article 22, see Broomhall, in: Triffterer/Ambos (eds.), *The Rome Statute of the International Criminal Court*, 3rd ed., 2016, Art. 22.

of the political organs of the UN) concerning previous, somewhat similar situations of the use of force.[297]

4. Perpetrators of the crime of aggression

a) Individual criminal responsibility

261   In line with Article 8 *bis* (1), according to which the crime of aggression may only be committed by "a person in a position effectively to exercise control over or to direct the political or military action of a State",[298] Article 25 (3) *bis* provides that, while the various forms of perpetration, as well as aiding and abetting, as foreseen in Article 25 (3), also apply with regard to the crime of aggression, any person to be eventually held criminally responsible with regard to the said crime by the Court must have been in a position required by both Article 8 *bis* (1) and Article 25 (3) *bis*.

b) Grounds for excluding criminal responsibility

262   Article 31 (1)(c) refers to the notion of self-defence as a possible ground excluding criminal responsibility under the Statute under specific narrow circumstances. Yet, this reference is only made so as to exclude criminal responsibility with regard to certain specific acts. Said provision does not, however, by the same token, also address the issue of inter-State self-defence under Article 51 of the UN Charter respectively under the applicable rule of customary international law. Moreover, to the extent military force is being used within the limits of Article 51 of the UN Charter respectively customary international law, such action does not amount to a violation of the UN Charter at all, and even less a manifest violation thereof which, therefore, *ipso facto*, excludes such action to even constitute an act of aggression within the meaning of Article 8 *bis* (2).

c) *Ne bis in idem*

263   Annex I, para. 7 of the enabling resolution adopted at the 2010 Review Conference (Resolution RC/Res.6) provides that the chapeau of Article 20 (3), as revised, will also refer to persons who have been tried by another court for conduct also "proscribed under article [...] 8 *bis*". They shall accordingly, as a matter of principle and subject to the *bona fide* character of the domestic proceedings as defined in Article 20 (3), not be tried by the Court with respect to the same conduct. This is true notwithstanding the adoption of Understanding no. 5 of the "Understandings regarding the amendments to the Rome Statute of the International Criminal Court on the crime of aggression", which *inter alia* provides that "the amendments [on the crime of aggression] shall not be interpreted as creating the [...] obligation to exercise domestic jurisdiction with respect to an act of aggression committed by another State". While it has been claimed that this Understanding aims at discouraging States from proceeding with domestic cases for the commission of the crime of aggression, the inclusion of a reference to Article 8 *bis* into the text of Article 20 (3) confirms, if there was need, that the principle of complementarity fully applies also when it comes to the crime of aggression. At the same time, the sole legal effect of any possible lack of genuine domestic proceedings under the principle of complementarity is that the ICC could then exercise its jurisdic-

---

[297] Schmalenbach, *JZ* 2010, 745 (747).
[298] See mns. 221 *et seq.*

tion; yet, to state the obvious, this does not amount to any form of legal obligation to prosecute any possible crime of aggression.

Given the fundamental distinction between *jus ad bellum* and *jus in bello* rules, it is **264** however only domestic proceedings addressing violations of the *jus ad bellum* amounting to a crime of aggression that can bar the Court from exercising its jurisdiction with regard to Article 8 *bis*.

d) Exercise of domestic jurisdiction over the crime of aggression

The exercise of the Court's jurisdiction with regard to the crime of aggression is, just **265** as with regard to the other crimes within the jurisdiction of the Court, governed by the principle of complementarity set out, in particular, in Article 17. In accordance, therewith, no. 5 of the "Understandings regarding the amendments to the Rome Statute of the International Criminal Court on the crime of aggression", adopted as part of the enabling Resolution RC/Res.6, underlines "that the amendments [*i.e.* Articles 8 *bis*, 15 *bis* and 15 *ter*] shall not be interpreted as creating the right or obligation to exercise domestic jurisdiction with respect to an act of aggression committed by another State".[299]

For one, the phrase confirms, if ever there had been need, that the principle of **266** complementarity underlying the Court's overall jurisdictional scheme, does not carry with it an implicit obligation to punish the respective crime, which crime is subject to the Court's complementary jurisdiction.[300] On the other hand, said formulation leaves it deliberately open, whether States are entitled or eventually even obliged, under general international law, to exercise their domestic criminal jurisdiction with regard to the crime of aggression committed by their own nationals, individuals other than their own nationals or, eventually, even exercise universal jurisdiction in that regard.

5. Relationship of the crime of aggression amendments with other parts of the Rome Statute

a) Replacing the "placeholder" on the crime of aggression

With the entry into force of the amendment on the crime of aggression in accordance **267** with (1) of the enabling Resolution RC/Res.6, Article 5 (2) of the Rome Statute lost its relevance. Article 5 (2) was the placeholder for the future inclusion of the crime of aggression into the Rome Statute. By Resolution ICC-ASP/16/Res.5 of 14 December 2017, the Assembly of State Parties decided to activate the Court's jurisdiction over the crime as of 17 July 2018. This jurisdiction, in accordance with article 5 para. 1, is subject to the temporal limitations laid down in Article 15 *bis*/*ter* (2).

b) Bearing on general international law

According to Article 10 of the Rome Statute, "[n]othing in this Part shall be **268** interpreted as limiting or prejudicing in any way existing or developing rules of international law for purposes other than this Statute". Understanding no. 4, as adopted by the 2010 Review Conference with regard to the amendment on the crime of aggression – and which ought to be taken into account as an additional tool of interpretation within the meaning of Article 31 (2)(b) of the Vienna Convention on

---

[299] RC/Res.6, Annex III, *Understandings Regarding the Amendments to the Rome Statute of the International Criminal Court on the Crime of Aggression*, para. 5.

[300] Werle and Jessberger, *Principles of International Criminal Law*, 3rd ed., 2014, 556.

the Law of Treaties -,[301] provides that Article 8 *bis* defining the crime of aggression (and accordingly also the underlying acts of aggression) ought to have no bearing on general international law. It provides that:

> *"It is understood that the amendments that address the definition of the act of aggression and the crime of aggression do so for the purpose of this Statute only. The amendments shall, in accordance with article 10 of the Rome Statute, not be interpreted as limiting or prejudicing in any way existing or developing rules of international law for purposes other than this Statute."*

269   Said understanding thus not only contains an explicit reference to Article 10 of the Rome Statute, but mirrors Article 10, reference to which can therefore be made.[302] Indeed given that Article 8 *bis*, containing the definition of the crime of aggression, was inserted into Part 2 of the Rome Statute, Understanding no. 4 is redundant since the very same effect is already reached by Article 10, which specifically refers to the interpretation of "this part" *i. e.* Part 2.

6. Outlook

270   Accordingly, Article 8 *bis* provides the definition of the act as well as the crime of aggression. Whereas at one point the definition of aggression could not be agreed upon by States, it eventually found its way relying heavily on the UN Charter and UN General Assembly Resolution 3314. Not only does it provide the definition, but also lists a non-exhaustive series of acts based on Resolution 3314.

271   Within the article, it provides definitions differentiating between the act of aggression and the crime of aggression. Additionally, it covers individual criminal responsibility for perpetrators of the crime of aggression.

272   At the time of the Kampala Review Conference, there was little divide in terms of providing the definition largely based on the two instruments, namely the UN Charter and UN General Assembly Resolution 3314.

---

[301] 1155 UNTS 331.

[302] See Triffterer/Heinze, in: Triffterer/Ambos (eds.), *The Rome Statute of the International Criminal Court*, 3rd ed., 2016, Art. 10, *passim*, in particular mn. 13.

IV.
TREATY-BASED JURISDICTION (ARTICLE 15 *BIS* OF THE ROME STATUTE)

Of the three different ways of triggering the Court's jurisdiction established under   **273**
Article 13, Article 15 *bis*, as introduced into the Statute as part of the Kampala
compromise on the crime of aggression, relates to Article 13 (a)-(c) only. Accordingly,
Article 15 *bis* deals with referrals by a State party and with *proprio motu* investigations
by the Prosecutor. Specific questions related to UN Security Council referrals in turn are
addressed in Article 15 *ter*, as far as the crime of aggression is concerned.

While the enabling Resolution RC/Res. 6, adopted at the 2010 Review Conference   **274**
"[r]ecall[s] paragraph 1 of Article 12 of the Rome Statute", it is worth noting that
Article 15 *bis* contains significant deviations from the regular jurisdictional scheme
underlying Article 12 of the Statute. This is a result of the long and difficult process of
finding an agreement on both, the definition of the crime of aggression as such and
the parameters, under which the court should eventually be in a position to exercise its
jurisdiction over the crime of aggression.

Article 15 *bis* also deviates from Article 5 (2) (*ante* Kampala), which stated that the   **275**
Court shall exercise its jurisdiction over the crime of aggression once a provision is
adopted in accordance with Articles 121 and 123 defining the crime and setting out the
conditions under which the Court shall exercise jurisdiction. While it would not have
been in accordance with the very wording of Article 5 to interpret it in the sense that a
mere adoption could have sufficed for the Court to be able to exercise its aggression-
related jurisdiction,[303] Resolution RC/Res.6 clarified, while being adopted under
Article 5 (2) of the Rome Statute, that the amendment and its entry into force is
governed by Article 121 (5).[304]

While the SWGCA, in preparation for the 2010 Review Conference, had formulated   **276**
only one draft for what was to become the current Article 8 *bis*, there were various
alternatives for what is now Article 15 *bis*. The most controversial question was whether
proceedings should possibly also be initiated by actors other than the UN Security
Council. The permanent members of the UN Security Council, as well as some other
States, had proposed that a determination by the UN Security Council under Article 39
of the UN Charter should be required for the exercise of the Court's jurisdiction.[305] This
position was opposed particularly by States that are members of the Non-Aligned
Movement. During the 2010 Review Conference, it became clear that the insistence on
a monopoly for the UN Security Council to trigger the Court's jurisdiction concerning
the crime of aggression would hinder any consensus to eventually be reached. The final
compromise, reached on the very last day of the Review Conference,[306] as now reflected

---

[303] For a more detailed discussion of the matter see Zimmermann, 10 *JICJ* 2012, 209 (212 *et seq.*); as
well as Clark, in: Triffterer/Ambos (eds.), *The Rome Statute of the International Criminal Court*, 3rd ed.,
2016, Art. 121, mns. 11 *et seq.*

[304] RC/Res. 6, para. 6, no. 1.

[305] For a more detailed discussion as to the drafting history of current Article 15 *bis* prior to the
Kampala Conference, *supra* mns. 51 *et seq.*; Werle and Jessberger, *Principles of International Criminal
Law*, 3rd ed., 2014, 546 *et seq.*; Ambos, *Treatise on International Criminal Law, Volume II*, 2014, 190
et seq.

[306] Barriga, in: Barriga and Kreß (eds.), *The Travaux Préparatoires of the Crime of Aggression*, 2012, 3 (32).

in Article 15 *bis*, therefore provides that it is not only the UN Security Council, but also States parties to the Statute and the Prosecutor that can initiate proceedings even with respect to an alleged crime of aggression.

277   Given its principled position on the matter, France, despite the fact of not having formally opposed the consensus leading to the adoption of Article 15 *bis*, still took the position in an explanatory declaration that "it cannot associate itself with [the] text as it disregards the relevant provisions of the UN Charter enshrined in Article 5 of the Rome Statute". According to France, Article 15 *bis*, as adopted, "restricts the role of the UN Security Council and contravenes the Charter of the United Nations under the terms of which the Security Council alone shall determine the existence of an act of aggression".[307]

278   In order to differentiate between proceedings triggered by States parties or *proprio motu* by the Prosecutor on the one hand and the UN Security Council on the other hand, as well as for the sake of clarity, it was decided to include, apart from Article 8 *bis* containing the substance of the crime of aggression, two separate additional Articles into the Rome Statute by way of an amendment: Article 15 *bis* dealing with State referrals and proceedings initiated by the Prosecutor *proprio motu*; and Article 15 *ter* covering UN Security Council referrals.

1. Exercise of jurisdiction

279   Article 15 *bis* (1) provides that "[t]he Court may exercise jurisdiction over the crime of aggression in accordance with article 13, paragraphs(a) and (c), subject to the provisions of this article."

280   Since Article 34 defines what is to be understood by "the Court", the introductory words of Article 15 *bis* (1) confirm, if there was any need, that accordingly all organs of the Court are subject to the jurisdictional limitations provided for by Article 15 *bis*.

281   Somewhat in contrast to Article 15 *bis* (3), the English version of Article 15 *bis* (1) further specifies that the Court may (rather than shall) exercise its jurisdiction if the respective requirements set out in Article 15 *bis* are fulfilled. It must be noted, however, that both the equally authentic French and Spanish texts refer in paras. 1 and 2 of Article 15 *bis* to the fact that the Court can exercise ("peut exercer"/"podrá ejercer") its jurisdiction in accordance with Article 13 (a) and (c). Thus the English "may" ought to be better understood as circumscribing the Court's ability ("can"/"peut"/"podrá") to exercise jurisdiction rather than providing some specific form of discretion beyond any discretion already otherwise provided for in the Statute.

282   By referring to the exercise of jurisdiction over the crime of aggression, Article 15 *bis* (1) also confirms that the underlying act of aggression, while in most, if not all, cases triggering State responsibility as a matter of general international law, is not the object of the proceedings before the Court as such. Nevertheless, the Court will obviously have to consider it, as well as possible grounds excluding the alleged illegality of any such underlying acts of aggression. It is indeed this interconnection that gave rise to the concerns as to the role of the UN Security Council. It stands to reason, however, that any determination by the Court that an act of aggression has been committed by organs of a State (eventually evoking those organs' individual criminal responsibility) cannot provide for any form of *de jure* binding effect as to the legal relations between the States

---

[307] Statement of France (with which the United States of America associated themselves) in explanation of position before the adoption of resolution RC/Res.6 on the crime of aggression, Review Conference of the Rome Statute of the International Criminal Court, Off. Rec., Annex VII, p. 122.

involved in the use of armed force, even if, *de facto* and politically, such a determination might be of relevance. This holds true despite the fact that there is no provision similar to Article 15 *bis* (9), which would *expressis verbis* exclude any such external effect of the Court's decisions for purposes of State responsibility.

In line with the compromise reached in Kampala, Article 15 *bis* (1) provides first that **283** "[t]he Court may exercise jurisdiction over the crime of aggression in accordance with Article 13, paragraphs (a) and (c)".[308] Article 15 *bis* therefore does not cover or regulate UN Security Council referrals, which are governed exclusively by Article 15 *ter* read in conjunction with, and subject to, Article 13 (b).

Yet, and to state the obvious, Article 16, enabling the UN Security Council to request **284** the Court not to commence respectively or to proceed with an investigation or prosecution, also applies to the crime of aggression when such an investigation or prosecution has been triggered by either a State party or *proprio motu* by the Prosecutor, as confirmed by Article 15 *bis* (8).[309]

Article 15 *bis* (1) further clarifies that, while acknowledging the possibility of State **285** referrals and investigations by the Prosecutor under Article 13 (a) and (c) respectively even when it comes to the crime of aggression, any such proceedings are subject to the specific requirements and conditions, as contained in Article 15 *bis* (2)–(10).

2. Jurisdiction *Ratione Temporis*

Article 15 *bis* (2) provides that **286**

> "[t]he Court may exercise jurisdiction only with respect to crimes of aggression committed one year after the ratification or acceptance of the amendments by thirty States Parties."

During the negotiation process, the issues related to the entry into force of the **287** amendment on the crime of aggression and the extent of the Court's jurisdiction *ratione temporis* concerning this crime proved to be among the most intricate and disputed ones. This lead to the solution now contained in Article 15 *bis* (2) and (3) (and further set out in Understanding no. 3), the compatibility of which with the amendment provisions of the Rome Statute remains, to say the least, however doubtful.[310] Likewise, the inter-relationship between Article 15 *bis* (2), Article 15 *bis* (3) and Understanding no. 3 is complex and bears significant legal difficulties.

While Article 15 *bis* (2) and (3) are inter-related (just as *mutatis mutandis* Article 15 **288** *ter* (2) and (3) concerning UN Security Council referrals), they still deal with different issues. It is to be noted at the outset, however, that neither of the two provisions (nor indeed the parallel provisions in Article 15 *ter* regulate the entry into force of the Kampala amendment as such. Rather, para. 1 of Resolution RC/Res.6 adopted at the 2010 Review Conference provides that the entry into force takes place in accordance with Article 121 (5), any doubts regarding the applicability of said provision notwithstanding.[311]

---

[308] As to the specific content of Article 13 (a) and (c) see Schabas and Pecorella, in: Triffterer/Ambos (eds.), *The Rome Statute of the International Criminal Court*, 3rd ed., 2016, Art. 13, mn. 15 and 20 respectively.

[309] As to details on Article 16, see Bergsmo, Pejic and Zhu, in: Triffterer/Ambos (eds.), *The Rome Statute of the International Criminal Court*, 3rd ed., 2016, Art. 16, *passim*.

[310] See generally Zimmermann, 10 *JICJ* 2012, 209, *passim*.

[311] For details see Zimmermann, 10 *JICJ* 2012, 209 *et seq.*, *passim*; McDougall, *The Crime of Aggression under the Rome Statute of the International Criminal Court*, 2013 252; Ambos, *Treatise on International Criminal Law, Volume II*, 2014, 216 *et seq.*

289   While Article 15 *bis* (2) regulates for which crimes of aggression the Court has jurisdiction *ratione temporis*, Article 15 *bis* (3) regulates the "activation" of the Court's aggression-related substance-matter jurisdiction.

290   Under Article 15 *bis* (2) (just like under Article 15 *ter* (2)), the Court will only be able to exercise its jurisdiction with respect to crimes of aggression "committed one year after the ratification or acceptance of the amendments by thirty States Parties". Put otherwise, Article 15 *bis* (2) circumscribes the Court's temporal jurisdiction rather than providing for the entry into force of the amendment or providing for the "activation" of the Court's jurisdiction concerning the crime of aggression. Article 15 *bis* (2) therefore constitutes a *lex specialis* to Article 11 (2) to the extent to which the issue is specifically governed by Article 15 *bis* (2).

291   The wording of Article 15 *bis* (2) ("[t]he Court may exercise jurisdiction") is identical to the introductory works of Article 15 *bis* (1) without raising any additional or separate issues of interpretation.[312]

292   It is worth noting, however, that unlike Article 24 (1) in relation to which Article 15 *bis* (2) (respectively Article 15 *ter* (2)) constitutes *lex specialis* which stipulates that "[n]o person shall be criminally responsible under this Statute for conduct prior to the entry into force of the Statute", Article 15 *bis* (2) (respectively Article 15 *ter* (2)) does not address the substantive criminal liability of the offender. Rather, it merely limits the Court's temporal jurisdiction. Notwithstanding this conceptual difference, the effect is the same, namely that a person committing a crime of aggression within the meaning of Article 8 *bis* prior to the critical date shall not face prosecution by the Court.

293   The phrase "with respect to crimes of aggression committed" confirms that it must be the specific crime of aggression, as set out in Article 8 *bis* (1), that must have taken place after the lapse of the one-year period after the 30th ratification or acceptance, rather than the underlying act of aggression, although in most cases, though not necessarily, both will coincide.

294   The wording of Article 15 *bis* (2) further confirms that the ratification of the Kampala amendment by thirty States and the additional lapse of a one-year period constituted a *conditio sine qua non* for the Court's exercise of its aggression-related temporal jurisdiction.

295   Article 15 *bis* (2), by specifically using the words "with respect to" rather than simply stating that the Court may only exercise its jurisdiction "one year after the ratification or acceptance of the amendments by thirty States Parties", indicates that the fulfilment of this condition defines the extent of the Court's temporal jurisdiction concerning the crime of aggression, namely those crimes committed one year after the 30th ratification or acceptance, as defined below.[313] Article 15 *bis* (2) therefore does not seem to define the time frame when such jurisdiction, once established, may be exercised. This latter question is then, under the Rome Statute as such, regulated by Article 15 *bis* (3). Put otherwise, under the wording of Article 15 *bis* (2), the Court can accordingly in principle also exercise its jurisdiction with respect to crimes committed prior to the decision provided for in Article 15 *bis* (3), but can effectively do so only after this decision was made.[314]

296   In order to fall within the Court's temporal jurisdiction, the respective crime of aggression (and thus also the underlying act of aggression) must have been committed, as Article 15 *bis* (2) confirms, at least one year after the ratification or acceptance of the

---

[312] See mn. 280.

[313] See *infra* mns. 299 *et seq.*

[314] As to the impact of Understanding no. 3 on this interpretation of Article 15 *bis* (2) see *infra* mns. 320 *et seq.*

amendments by thirty States parties. Yet, at least certain of the acts of aggression defined in Article 8 *bis* (2), such as Article 8 *bis* (2)(a) 2nd alternative ("any military occupation, however temporary, resulting from such invasion or attack") or (2)(g) 2nd alternative ("any extension of their presence [*i.e.* the presence of troops] in such [foreign] territory beyond the termination of the agreement"), are of a continuous character within the meaning of Article 14 (2) of the ILC's ARSIWA, *i.e.* the breach of the obligation "extends over the entire period during which the act continues and remains not in conformity with the international obligation".[315]

While said standard has primarily been developed for purposes of State responsibility, **297** it nevertheless has also been adopted, albeit reluctantly, for purposes of international criminal law.[316] Given the nature of the abovementioned acts of aggression, individuals might very well come within the Court's jurisdiction *ratione temporis* with regard to the commission of the crime of aggression provided the commission of the (continuous) act of aggression itself occurred within the jurisdictional reach *ratione temporis* of the Court.

It is noteworthy that Article 15 *bis* (2) (just like Article 15 *ter* (2)), contrary to the **298** wording of Article 121 (4) and (5), refers to the "ratification or acceptance" of the amendments by thirty States parties rather than to the deposit of an instrument of ratification or acceptance. This difference in wording, even if its drafters might eventually have thought to use a formula which was only shorter yet was meant to be identical in content, could also be perceived as implying that any such "ratification/ acceptance" refers to the amendment becoming binding for the ratifying/accepting State, rather than referring to the act of depositing the instrument of ratification or acceptance. Under Article 121 (5) however, any such ratification/acceptance only takes effect one year after the deposit of the instrument of ratification/acceptance.

It is not entirely clear what Article 15 *bis* (2) means when it refers to the **299** "acceptance" of the amendments alongside a possible "ratification". At the time of writing, 38 States have so far acceded to the amendment on the crime of aggression by submitting a formal declaration to the depositary: Andorra, Argentina, Austria, Belgium, Botswana, Chile, Costa Rica, Croatia, Cyprus, the Czech Republic, El Salvador, Estonia, Finland, Georgia, Germany, Guyana, Iceland, Ireland, Latvia, Liechtenstein, Lithuania, Luxembourg, Malta, the Netherlands, North Macedonia, Panama, Paraguay, Poland, Portugal, Samoa, San Marino, Slovakia, Slovenia, Spain, the State of Palestine, Switzerland, Trinidad and Tobago and Uruguay.[317] It is thus beyond doubt that these ratifications meet the quorum required by Article 15 *bis* (2) (respectively by Article 15 *ter* (2)).

Besides, thirteen States[318] have acceded to the Rome Statute after the Kampala **300** amendment on the crime of aggression had been adopted, *i.e.* after 11 June 2010,[319]

---

[315] UN DOC A/56/83, 12 December 2001.

[316] See Pangalangan, in: Triffterer/Ambos (eds.), *The Rome Statute of the International Criminal Court*, 3rd ed., 2016, Art. 24, mns. 13 *et seq.*

[317] See https://treaties.un.org/pages/ViewDetails.aspx?src=TREATY&mtdsg_no=XVIII-10-b&chapter= 18&clang=_en (last accessed May 2019).

[318] See as to the question of Palestinian statehood and the status of Palestine vis-à-vis the Rome Statute generally Zimmermann, 11 *JICJ* 2013, 303 *et seq.*, *passim*; see also the depositary note concerning Palestine, CN.12.2015.TREATIES-XVIII.13, 2 January 2015, as well as the communications by Canada, 23 January 2015, https://treaties.un.org/doc/Publication/CN/2015/CN.62.2015-Eng.pdf (last accessed May 2019); by the United States of America, 23 January 2015, https://treaties.un.org/doc/Publication/CN/ 2015/CN.64.2015-Eng.pdf (last accessed May 2019); and by Israel, 23 January 2015, https://treaties.un. org/doc/Publication/CN/2015/CN.63.2015-Eng.pdf (last accessed May 2019).

[319] These States include Cabo Verde, Côte d'Ivoire, Grenada, Guatemala, Maldives, Moldova, Philippines (having meanwhile declared its withdrawal from the Statute in March 2019), Seychelles, St. Lucia, Tunisia,

without expressing an intention not to be bound by the treaty, as amended. Only two States, Palestine and El Salvador (the first one with over one year in between), have both ratified the Rome Statute after the Kampala Diplomatic Conference, as well as ratified or acceded to the amendment on the crime of aggression.

301   The wording of Article 15 *bis* (2) (and the parallel wording of Article 15 *ter* (2)) refers to the fact that "[t]he Court may exercise jurisdiction only with respect to crimes of aggression committed one year after the ratification or acceptance of the amendments by thirty States Parties". This raises two questions: for one, has a State, ratifying the Rome Statute after 11 June 2010, thereby also automatically accepted the Kampala amendment, and, secondly, can such a State then accordingly be also counted towards the necessary quorum of thirty States? Though the quorum has in fact already been reached by accession to the amendment itself, these questions might still be of huge interest for States wondering about the exact content of their contractual obligations.

302   In that regard, it is worth recalling preambular paragraph 3 of Resolution RC/Res.5, also adopted in 2010 Review Conference, and dealing with the amendments to Article 8 of the Rome Statute. The said provision specifically "[c]onfirm[ed] that, in light of the provision of Article 40 (5) of the Vienna Convention on the Law of Treaties, States that subsequently become States Parties to the Statute will be allowed to decide whether to accept the amendment contained in this resolution at the time of ratification, acceptance or approval of, or accession to the Statute". In contrast thereto, Resolution RC/Res.6, dealing with the crime of aggression, contains no such provision. Yet, given that the principle underlying Article 40 (5) of the Vienna Convention on the Law of Treaties constitutes customary international law,[320] it still applies, the lack of any specific reference to Article 40 (5) notwithstanding. As a matter of fact, at least those States that have ratified the Rome Statute after the Kampala amendment on the crime of aggression has entered into force for the first State have thus, to use the formula contained in Article 40 (5) of the Vienna Convention on the Law of Treaties, "become parties to the treaty after the entry into force of the amending agreement".[321] This is due to the fact that, as shown,[322] the entry into force of the Kampala amendment on the crime of aggression is not governed by the jurisdictional clauses contained in Article 15 *bis* (2) and (3) (respectively in Article 15 *ter* (2) and (3)), but rather by Article 121 (5). It thus seems that at least those States that have (or will have) ratified the Rome Statute after that date ought to be counted towards the amendment-accepting States unless they have expressed a different intention, in line with Article 40 (5) of the Vienna Convention on the Law of Treaties.

303   This understanding is confirmed by the fact that Article 15 (2) specifically refers to the "ratification or acceptance of the amendments", an *ex post* ratification of the amendment then being a specific form of acceptance under Article 40 (5) of the Vienna Convention on the Law of Treaties. In fact, none of the States that ratified the Rome Statute after the Kampala review conference has submitted a declaration expressing an intention not to be considered as a party to the amended treaty within the meaning of the said Article 40 (5). Accordingly, such States will then, just like States that had

---

Vanuatu and most recently the State of Palestine and El Salvador, see https://treaties.un.org/pages/ViewDetails.aspx?src=TREATY&mtdsg_no=XVIII-10&chapter=18&clang=_en (last accessed May 2019).

[320] See for such proposition *inter alia* Villiger, *Commentary on the 1969 Vienna Convention on the Law of Treaties*, 2009, Art. 40, mn. 15.

[321] McDougall, *The Crime of Aggression under the Rome Statute of the International Criminal Court*, 2013, 265.

[322] See *supra* mns. 288.

become parties prior to the entry into force of Articles 8 *bis*, 15 *bis* and 15 *ter*, also have the right to opt out from the Court's jurisdiction on the crime of aggression under Article 15 *bis* (4), provided such opting-out is still necessary anyhow.[323]

It is true that the wording of Article 15 *bis* (2) (just like that of Article 15 *ter* (2)) **304** specifically refers to the "ratification or acceptance of the amendments by thirty States parties" rather than to the acceptance by thirty States *tout court*. Yet, Article 2 (1)(g) of the Vienna Convention on the Law of Treaties defines a "[State] party" as "a State which has consented to be bound by the treaty and for which the treaty is in force". This might be understood as also comprising newly acceding States.

On the other hand, it seems that delegations participating in the Kampala Con- **305** ference, when using the formula "[t]he Court may exercise jurisdiction only with respect to crimes of aggression committed one year after the ratification or acceptance of the amendments by thirty States Parties" in Article 15 *bis* (2), simply meant to replicate the wording of Article 121 (4) and (5), which refer to the point in time after instruments of ratification or acceptance have been deposited. It thus seems that the drafters of Article 15 *bis* (2) (and of Article 15 *ter* (2)) omitted the reference to the deposition of instruments only to be more concise rather than to convey another meaning, as outlined above. Yet, this intention is neither reflected in the *travaux préparatoires* of the provision, nor in the text itself.

The contrary position, namely that thirty States needed to formally ratify or accept **306** the amendments as such, rather than either ratify or accede to the amended treaty *in toto,* in order for the amendments to become applicable, stands in line, however, with a press communiqué distributed by the ICC on the occasion of San Marino's ratification of the amendment on the crime of aggression, which stated that "[t]he Court may exercise jurisdiction over the crime of aggression once thirty States Parties have ratified the amendments"[324] instead of using the more precise terminology "ratified or accepted" formula used in Article 15 *bis* (and in Article 15 *ter*) (2).

This somewhat more restrictive position also seems to be shared by the depositary, **307** the UN Secretary General. More specifically, the UN Secretary General has taken the position that new parties to the Statute must explicitly ratify the amendments, or are otherwise deemed to be party to the original 1998 version of the Rome Statute as agreed upon in Rome only.[325]

In the end, this discussion turned out to be rather theoretical, as the necessary **308** number of ratifications of the amendment had been submitted by 2016. Nonetheless, the very same issue might still be relevant for yet another purpose.

At least when taken at face value and leaving aside Understanding no. 3 for the time **309** being,[326] Article 15 *bis* (2) determines the earliest point in time with regard to which the Court may exercise its aggression-related treaty-based jurisdiction, namely covering all such crimes "committed one year after the ratification or acceptance of the amendments by thirty States Parties". Accordingly, provided one were to share the position that States acceding to the Statute post-Kampala were to be counted towards the quorum of thirty States, the ASP Resolution ICC-ASP/16/Res.5 of 14 December 2017 (being silent

---

[323] In detail, see *infra* at mns. 359 *et seq.*

[324] Press Release No. ICC-ASP-20141119-PR1065, Assembly of States Parties to the International Criminal Court, 19 November 2014, see http://www.icc-cpi.int/en_menus/icc/press%20and%20media/press%20releases/Pages/PR1065.aspx (last accessed May 2019).

[325] *Cf. e. g.* the depositary notification for Cote d'Ivoire, referring to the Rome Statute as agreed upon in Rome on 17 July 1998: https://treaties.un.org/doc/Publication/CN/2013/CN.150.2013-Eng.pdf (last accessed May 2019).

[326] On the relevance of Understanding no. 3 as to the activation of the Court's jurisdiction see *infra* mns. 320 *et seq.*

on this issue) under Article 15 *bis* (3) might have retroactively activated the Court's jurisdiction *ratione temporis* for crimes of aggression committed in 2014, *i. e.* after thirty States had become bound by the Kampala amendment including those States that ratified the Statute after the Kampala amendment had already entered into force.

3. Activation of the Court's treaty-based, aggression-related jurisdiction

310   Article 15 *bis* (3) provides that

"[t]he Court shall exercise jurisdiction over the crime of aggression in accordance with this article, subject to a decision to be taken after 1 January 2017 by the same majority of States Parties as is required for the adoption of an amendment to the Statute."

311   Leaving aside once again the complexities of the amendment process leading to the adoption of the amendment on the crime of aggression at the 2010 Review Conference, which puts into question its compatibility with regular rules of the law of treaties,[327] Article 15 *bis* (3) (as well as Article 15 *ter* (3) regarding the Court's UN Security Council-based jurisdiction) provides that the Court may only exercise its aggression-related jurisdiction once a decision has been taken to that effect after 1 January 2017 by the same majority of States parties as is required for the adoption of an amendment to the Rome Statute.

312   This has rightly been described as an "activation" of the Court's aggression-related jurisdiction which might thus be considered existing, but still "dormant" pending this very decision. In a way, that situation was thus somewhat similar to the one prior to the entry into force of the Kampala amendment under Article 5 (1)(d) and (2) as it then stood, which provided that while the Court already had jurisdiction over the crime of aggression from the very beginning of its existence, it could not yet exercise it.[328]

a) Activation post-adoption of the Kampala amendments

313   The use of the word "shall" in Article 15 *bis* (3) as compared to the "may" in paras. 1, 2 and 5 of Article 15 *bis* ("ejercerá"/"podráejercer" in Spanish; "peut exercer"/"exerce" in French) seems to imply that, once the decision has been made under Article 15 *bis* (3), the Court is duty-bound to exercise its jurisdiction, obviously subject to those statutory rules governing such an exercise of jurisdiction.

314   As in (1), (2) and (4) of Article 15 *bis*, (3) once again reconfirms that the Court will only exercise jurisdiction *vis-à-vis* natural persons allegedly having committed a crime of aggression (rather than exercising jurisdiction concerning alleged acts of aggression).[329]

315   The wording of Article 15 *bis* (3) further clarifies and once more confirms that any exercise of jurisdiction over the crime of aggression shall take place in accordance with Article 15 *bis* as constituting *lex specialis* to the regular jurisdictional rules also contained in the Statute.

316   Article 15 *bis* (3) further provides that in order to "activate" the Court's jurisdiction, a positive decision in that regard had to be taken after 1 January 2017. Under

---

[327] Zimmermann, 10 *JICJ* 2012, 209.
[328] For further details *supra* mn. 82.
[329] See mns. 100, 201 *et seq.*

the wording of Article 15 *bis* (3), the purpose of the provision is not to regulate the Court's temporal jurisdiction (that question being decided by Article 15 *bis* (2)), but rather to determine only from what point onwards the Court ought to actually exercise its jurisdiction.

The formula "subject to a decision" contained in Article 15 *bis* (3) (as well as in 15 **317** *ter* (3)) implied, however, that the States parties might decide otherwise, *i.e.* might have provided that the Court shall not have jurisdiction for acts of aggression eventually committed in the period between the 30th ratification has become effective and the point in time the decision under (3) was taken (if ever there was such period at all).

The last part of Article 15 *bis* (3), by using the phrase "the same majority of States **318** Parties as is required for the adoption of an amendment to the Statute", makes reference to Article 121 (3).[330] Accordingly, any decision under Article 15 *bis* (3) to activate the Court's jurisdiction required a positive decision by two thirds of the States parties to the Rome Statute, in accordance with Article 121 (3) rather than a two-thirds majority of those States present and voting when any such decision is to be taken. The term "States Parties" in this context is referring to the *then* current number of States parties rather than to the current number of States parties.

The decision in question, just like the adoption of an amendment, could have either **319** been taken at a meeting of the Assembly of States Parties or, should the opportunity arise, at a Review Conference. The first way turned out to be chosen: On 14 December 2017, after two weeks of meetings of the 16th ASP in New York City, by Resolution ICC-ASP/16/Res.5 the ASP by consensus

> "[d]ecide[d] to activate the Court's jurisdiction over the crime of aggression as of 17 July 2018".[331]

b) Jurisdiction *ratione temporis*, activation of the Court's jurisdiction and Understanding no. 3

The already complex questions of the Court's temporal jurisdiction on the one hand **320** and of the "activation" of its aggression-related jurisdiction on the other, as laid out in Article 15 *bis/ter* (2) (regulating the former) and in Article 15 *bis/ter* (3) (regulating the latter), is further complicated by the terms of Understanding no. 3, adopted by the negotiating States in Kampala as Annex III of the enabling Resolution RC/Res. 6, whereby the Kampala amendment on the crime of aggression was adopted. This understanding provides in quite unequivocal terms:

> "It is understood that in case of article 13, paragraph (a) or (c), the Court may exercise its jurisdiction only with respect to crimes of aggression committed after a decision in accordance with article 15 bis, paragraph 3, is taken, and one year after the ratification or acceptance of the amendments by thirty States Parties, whichever is later."

In that regard, one has to first note that by making reference to Article 13, (a) or (c) **321** only, the understanding was meant to only govern the Court's treaty-based aggression-related jurisdiction, a fact further confirmed by the exclusive reference in the text of Understanding no. 3 to Article 15 *bis* (3) (but not to Article 15 *ter* (3)).[332]

---

[330] On Article 121 (3) see Clark, in: Triffterer/Ambos (eds.), *The Rome Statute of the International Criminal Court*, 3rd ed., 2016, Art. 121, mn. 9; Werle and Jessberger, *Principles of International Criminal Law*, 3rd ed., 2014, 555.

[331] Resolution ICC-ASP/16/Res.5, 14 December 2017, operative para. 1.

[332] As to the parallel provision in Article 15 *ter infra* mn. 416.

322   Moreover, the Understanding reversed the effect of the quorum provided for in Article 15 *bis* (2) on the one hand[333] and of the decision referred to in Article 15 *bis* (3) on the other[334] as proscribed by the two provisions.

323   With regard to the former, the text of the Understanding, contrary to the content of Article 15 *bis* (2), foresees that the Court may only exercise its jurisdiction a year after the ratification or acceptance of the amendments by thirty States parties. It thus seems that the said Understanding, contrary to the wording of Article 15 *bis* (2) (which instead uses the phrase "with respect to") provides for a definite time frame for the exercise of jurisdiction by the Court, rather than circumscribing the extent of the Court's temporal jurisdiction. This is true notwithstanding the heading of Understanding no. 3, which refers to "[j]urisdiction *ratione temporis*".

324   With regard to the latter, *i.e.* Article 15 *bis* (3), it provides that the Court's jurisdiction *ratione temporis* is limited in that "the Court may exercise its jurisdiction only with respect to crimes of aggression committed after a decision in accordance with Article 15 *bis*, paragraph 3, is taken". This stands, once again, in contrast to the actual wording of Article 15 *bis* (3) which, as shown above,[335] conversely merely regulates the exercise, by the Court of its jurisdiction rather than circumscribing its temporal jurisdiction.

325   Given that, at best, the said Understanding constitutes an agreement relating to the text of the amendment made in connection with the conclusion of the treaty within the meaning of Article 32 (2)(a) of the Vienna Convention on the Law of Treaties, it may only serve as an interpretative tool, which may not, however, set aside the clear text of the treaty as such. It is thus submitted that the Understanding's aim was only to further define what was previously agreed upon while not limiting the effect of Article 15 *bis* (2) and (3), respectively. Put otherwise, the temporal limitations as to the reach of the Court's temporal jurisdiction (as laid down in Article 15 *bis* (2)), and as to the *exercise* of such jurisdiction (as laid down in Article 15 *bis* (3)) stand unabated while Understanding no. 3 added further limitations, as set out above.

326   Thus, on the whole and taking the combined effect of Article 15 *bis* (2), Article 15 *bis* (3) and Understanding no. 3 into account,

– the Court only became able to exercise its jurisdiction one year after the 30ᵗʰ ratification or acceptance had become effective[336] and after the decision contemplated in Article 15 *bis* (3) was made
and

– the Court's jurisdiction can only be exercised with respect to crimes of aggression committed after the 30ᵗʰ ratification or acceptance has become effective and after the decision provided for in Article 15 *bis* (3) had been made.

4. The "opt-out" option of the Kampala amendment

327   Article 15 *bis* (4) provides that

> "[t]he Court may, in accordance with Article 12, exercise jurisdiction over a crime of aggression, arising from an act of aggression committed by a State Party, unless that State Party has previously declared that it does not accept such jurisdiction by lodging a declaration with the Registrar. The withdrawal of such a declaration may be effected at any time and shall be considered by the State Party within three years."

---

[333] See mns. 286 *et seq.*
[334] See mns. 310 *et seq.*
[335] See *supra* mn. 289.
[336] See mns. 294 *et seq.*

The introductory words of Article 15 *bis* (4) are identical to those words used in **328** Article 15 *bis* (1). Both phrases should thus be interpreted in the same manner, *i.e.* as merely circumscribing the extent of the Court's jurisdiction,[337] where this particular provision is concerned with the Court's jurisdiction *ratione personae*.

Article *15 bis* (4) uses the words "in accordance with Article 12", providing that, as a **329** matter of principle, the general rules governing the Court's exercise of jurisdiction as enshrined in Article 12[338] also apply when it comes to the crime of aggression. However, this is subject to the extent to which Article 15 *bis* constitutes a *lex specialis*.

Subject to a State party's exercise of the opt-out possibility provided for in Article 15 **330** *bis* (4), a State that is a contracting party is, under Article 12 (1), thus deemed to have accepted the Court's jurisdiction also with regard to the crime of aggression, as contained in Article 5 (1) (d),[339] regardless of whether it has, in one way or the other, specifically accepted the Kampala amendments on the crime of aggression.

Accordingly, the Court is thus, as a matter of principle and subject to Article 15 *bis* **331** (5),[340] in a position to first exercise its treaty-based aggression-related jurisdiction with regard to crimes of aggression committed on either the territory of a State party or committed against vessels or aircraft registered in a State party, provided that in any case the said State party is subject to the Court's aggression-related jurisdiction. In the latter respect, *i.e.* concerning possible crimes of aggression committed against vessels or aircraft registered in a State party, it is particularly worth noting that under Article 8 *bis* (2)(d) even the attack against the sea or air forces, or the marine and air fleets of another State can amount to the crime of aggression.[341]

Besides, under Article 12 (2) (b), the Court may also, again subject to both **332** Article 15 *bis* (5) and the opting-out option available to States parties, exercise its treaty-based aggression-related jurisdiction provided the accused is a national of a State party.

Article 12 (3) enables States, which are not parties to the Statute, to accept the **333** exercise of jurisdiction by the Court with respect to the crime in question, by way of a declaration lodged with the ICC Registrar. However, in line with Rule 44 of the Court's Rules of Procedure and Evidence, Article 12 (3) has to be understood as an acceptance of jurisdiction with regard to an overall situation and with respect to all "crimes referred to in Article 5 of relevance to the situation'.

In that regard it seems to be in line with the object and purpose of Article 15 *bis* **334** (5), namely to protect third States, not parties to the Rome Statute to also allow Article 12 (3) declarations to apply to the crime of aggression, the categorical wording of Article 15 (5) "the Court shall not exercise its jurisdiction" notwithstanding. Moreover, given the interpretation of Article 12 (3), as laid down in Rule 44 of the Rules of Procedure and Evidence, any such declaration does also entail the acceptance of the Court's treaty-based aggression-related jurisdiction by the State making the declaration.

Given the unequivocal wording of Article 12 (3), which only refers to States which are **335** not parties to this Statute as eventually making such declarations, it does not apply as

---

[337] See mn. 281.

[338] For further details see Schabas and Pecorella, in: Triffterer/Ambos (eds.), *The Rome Statute of the International Criminal Court*, 3rd ed., 2016; Art. 12, *passim; Ambos, Treatise on International Criminal Law, Volume II*, 2014, 219.

[339] McDougall, *The Crime of Aggression under the Rome Statute of the International Criminal Court*, 2013, 254; Kreß and von Holtzendorff, 8 JICJ 2010, 1179 (1213).

[340] See *infra* mns. 391 *et seq.*

[341] For details *supra* mns. 153 *et seq.*

such to "non-accepting" States parties which have not accepted the Court's treaty-based, aggression-related jurisdiction under Article 15 *bis* (4) read in light of the ASP decision activating the Court's aggression-related jurisdiction. At the same time, there appears to be no reason why a State should not be permitted to partially withdraw its opting-out declaration by means of an *ad hoc* declaration in accordance with the idea underlying Article 12 (3).

336   Once again, the introductory words of Article 15 *bis* (4) ("exercise jurisdiction over a crime of aggression") are identical to the ones used in Article 15 *bis* (1), reference to which[342] is therefore made.

337   Under Article 15 *bis* (4), the initiation of proceedings requires the aggressor State's consent. As a matter of principle, Article 15 *bis* (4) therefore provides for the Court's treaty-based, aggression-related jurisdiction only if the underlying act of aggression has been, as the provision puts it, "committed by a State party". Accordingly, the said act of aggression, as defined in Article 8 *bis* (2), must be attributable to a State party to the Rome Statute under the regular rules of State responsibility as they have been codified in the ILC's ARSIWA. For the purposes of Article 15 *bis* (4) it therefore does not matter whether such a State party has ratified or otherwise accepted[343] the Kampala amendments on the crime of aggression, unless such a State party has not accepted the Court's treaty-based, aggression-related jurisdiction.[344]

338   The crime of aggression must furthermore "arise from" ("résultant d'un acte d'agression" in the French version of the text and "resultante de un acto de agresión" in the Spanish text) an act of aggression attributable to a State party that has accepted the Court's aggression-related jurisdiction. Article 15 *bis* (4) does not require, however, that the act of aggression is then necessarily committed by a national of a State party. Indeed, there might be scenarios in which the act of aggression (rather than the crime of aggression) is committed by nationals of third States, but where the act is nevertheless attributable to a State party bound by the amendments, *e.g.* under Article 8 of the ILC's ARSIWA. Provided that the crime of aggression was then committed by nationals of a State party bound by the amendments and occurred on the territory of such a State, the Court is in a position to exercise its treaty-based, aggression-related jurisdiction.

339   Article 15 *bis* (4) presupposes the consent of States parties to the Court's exercise of its treaty-based, aggression-related jurisdiction. However, under Article 15 *bis* (4) as adopted in Kampala, a State party has the option to declare that it does not accept the Court's treaty-based jurisdiction over the crime of aggression by lodging a declaration with the ICC Registrar. This provision is remarkable, given its absence in the likewise newly introduced Article 8 (2)(e)(xiii), (xiv) and (xv) of the Rome Statute. The establishment of such an opt-out procedure for the crime of aggression became a necessary negotiation strategy during the Kampala Review Conference, aiming mainly at convincing France and Great Britain to stop insisting on the monopoly of the UN Security Council when it comes to the crime of aggression.[345]

340   Yet, this compromise, as enshrined in the opt-out procedure, is hardly, if at all, compatible with Article 121 (5), which under the enabling resolution adopted at the Kampala Review Conference constitutes the treaty provision providing for the entry into force of the Kampala amendments, and which states that amendments only apply

---

[342] See mns. 279 *et seq.*
[343] For detail as to this question, see mns. 299 *et seq.*
[344] Kreß and von Holtzendorff, 8 *JICJ* 2010, 1179 (1213).
[345] Kreß and von Holtzendorff, 6 *Vereinte Nationen* 2010, 260 (262); Ambos, *Treatise on International Criminal Law, Volume II*, 2014, 193.

vis-à-vis those States parties which have accepted them.[346] As a matter of fact, Article 15 *bis* (4) attempted to force States which are not willing to accept the Court's treaty-based, aggression-related jurisdiction to formally opt out of this jurisdiction, instead of simply allowing them to remain silent and rely on their non-acceptance of the amendment. Put otherwise, once the conditions of Article 15 *bis* (2) and (3) were fulfilled, the amendment were supposed to enter into force for all States parties except those that submitted an opting-out declaration, making it thus *mutatis mutandis* (but for the opting-out option) subject to the amendment procedure provided for in Article 124 (4).

Given the doubts about the compatibility of the opting-out procedure as laid down   341
in the Kampala amendments with the amendment provisions of the Rome Statute, States could, at any given moment prior to the critical date, have made declarations taking just this position. By the same token, they could have indicated that they therefore did not feel the need to formally lodge an opt-out declaration, in order not to be bound by the amendment, given that Article 121 (5) has to be interpreted just in this manner.

a) Opt-out declarations

aa) Scope *ratione personae* of opt-out declarations

The opt-out option as it was foreseen in Article 15 *bis* (4), was meant to apply to all   342
States parties to the Rome Statute, irrespective of whether they had previously ratified the amendment, had otherwise accepted it by ratifying the Statute after the amendment had already been adopted,[347] or finally had not accepted the Kampala amendments at all.[348]

There is no hint in the text of Article 15 *bis* (4) that would prevent even a State that   343
has itself participated in bringing about the "activation" of the Court's treaty-based, aggression-related jurisdiction by way of its ratification or acceptance from "protecting" its own citizens from the Court's jurisdiction by submitting an opting-out declaration to the Registrar in accordance with Article 15 *bis* (4).

In contrast thereto, the opting-out option under Article 15 *bis* (4) is not available to   344
non-States parties, them already being protected against the Court exercising its treaty-based, aggression-related jurisdiction *vis-à-vis* their nationals or concerning acts on their territory by virtue of Article 15 *bis* (5).

bb) Timing and effects *ratione temporis* of opt-out declarations

Opt-out declarations under Article 15 *bis* (4) could be lodged with the Registrar even   345
before the Court's treaty-based, aggression-related jurisdiction has been activated under Article 15 *bis* (2) and (3),[349] and might indeed also accompany a notification of ratification of the Kampala amendments.[350]

It is not, however, beyond doubt whether the term "previously" refers to a point in   346
time prior to the commission of an act of aggression, or rather to one prior to the exercise, by the Court, of its jurisdiction in a given case. However, the very structure of the text, which links the declaration to the commission of the act of aggression, seems to

---

[346] For further details see Zimmermann, 10 *JICJ* 2012, 209 (220 *et seq.*); Ambos, 53 *GYbIL* 2010, 463 (504); Schmalenbach, *JZ* 2010, 745 (750 *et seq.*).

[347] See for such possibility *supra* mns. 299 *et seq.*

[348] Clark, 2 *GoJIL* 2010, 689 (704); McDougall, *The Crime of Aggression under the Rome Statute of the ICC*, 2013, 253.

[349] For details see mns. 286 *et seq.*

[350] See also mn. 299.

militate in favour of an interpretation requiring the declaration to be made prior to the act of aggression rather than to the exercise of jurisdiction by the Court.[351] It is also only this interpretation, which is fully in line with the object and purpose of the provision. Were it otherwise, a State could commit an act of aggression and would, if the Court started an investigation, subsequently still be able to bar the Court from exercising its jurisdiction, almost until the very last minute before proceedings are about to begin. Nonetheless, given that Article 15 *bis* (4) does not contain any precise deadline, no specific period of time has to lapse between the point in time at which the declaration is made and the time during which the act of aggression takes place, in order for the former to be effective.

347   In order to prevent States from misusing the opt-out option, a certain minimum period of time is however required before such a declaration becomes effective, thereby ensuring that the opt-out did not occur with the specific plan in mind to commit an act of aggression within the immediate future. As a matter of fact, to paraphrase the ICJ in its *Nicaragua* judgment concerning the right of a State to denounce a declaration under Article 36 (2) ICJ Statute accepting the jurisdiction of the ICJ, it appears from the requirement of good faith that such unilateral declarations should be treated, by analogy, according to the law of treaties, which requires a reasonable time for withdrawal even when it comes to treaties that contain no provision regarding the duration of their validity.[352] The necessary time to have lapsed before any such opting out becomes effective would then depend on the circumstances of the specific case.

348   In the normal course of events, lodging such a declaration in the immediate temporal context of an act of aggression with the intent to prevent the Court from exercising jurisdiction in this case, will not, however, fulfil the definition of the crime of aggression's planning and preparation phase.[353] As a matter of fact, the sole aim of such opting out might simply be to avoid having the use of force by one State, albeit eventually a controversial one, not being exposed to judicial scrutiny rather than pursuing a plan to commit the crime of aggression.

349   Despite the fact that an opt-out declaration under Article 15 (4) 2ⁿᵈ sentence concerning the Court's treaty-based, aggression-related jurisdiction may be made for an unlimited period of time, it could still from the very beginning be made, if a State party wishes, for a limited time period, given that it can also be revoked at any time.[354]

cc) Breadth of declarations made

350   Article 15 *bis* (4) further raises the issue of whether an opt-out declaration can also be limited to one of the jurisdictional links provided for in Article 12, *i. e.* the nationality of the perpetrator or the place of the offence. Unlike Article 124, the very wording of which refers to declarations, pursuant to which either war crimes committed by a State party's nationals or those committed on its territory (or both) may be excluded from the jurisdiction of the Court, Article 15 *bis* (4) refers generally to the Court's jurisdiction "over a crime of aggression, arising from an act of aggression committed by a State Party" that may be excluded by way of an opting-out declaration. This might at first glance invite an *e contrario* argument. On the other hand, one has to take into account

---

[351] Ambos, 53 *GYbIL* 2010, 463 (505); Reisinger Coracini, 2 *GoJIL* 2010, 745 (777).

[352] See *mutatis mutandis ICJ, Military and Paramilitary Activities in and against Nicaragua (Nicaragua v. United States of America)*, Judgment (Jurisdiction of the Court and Admissibility of the Application), ICJ Rep. 1984, 392, 419, para. 63, as well as *ICJ, Land and Maritime Boundary between Cameroon and Nigeria (Cameroon v. Nigeria: Equatorial Guinea intervening)*, Judgment (Preliminary Objections), ICJ Rep. 1998, 275, 295, para. 33.

[353] But see for a somewhat different position Reisinger Coracini, 2 *GoJIL* 2010, 745 (777).

[354] On this issue see *infra* mn. 352.

the fact that an opting-out declaration under Article 15 *bis* (4) limits the Court's otherwise existing treaty-based, aggression-related jurisdiction. It thus seems to be appropriate to also allow for a more limited opting-out declaration to be made under Article 15 *bis* (4),[355] third parties being protected anyhow by virtue of Article 15 *bis* (5).

dd) Addressee of opt-out declarations

Article 15 *bis* (4) expressly states that any opt-out declaration ought to be lodged with **351** the ICC Registrar. This stands in contrast to possible opting-out declarations to be made under Article 124, which is silent on the matter and in reliance on which the only two declarations made so far under Article 124 were both addressed to the depositary rather than to the ICC Registrar.[356]

b) Withdrawal of opt-out declarations

As the text of Article 15 *bis* (4) 2nd sentence unequivocally confirms, and given the **352** character of an opting-out declaration as a unilateral act limiting the obligations of a State party arising under the Statute it may, just like generally reservations to treaties under the law of treaties and declarations made under Article 124,[357] be withdrawn at any time.

Given that the opting-out declaration has to be lodged, under Article 15 *bis* (4) **353** 1st sentence, with the Court's Registrar, the *actus contrarius* of withdrawing such a declaration would then also have to be addressed to the Registrar. This is *mutatis mutandis* confirmed by the practice under Article 124, as France, which had previously made a declaration under Article 124, in 2008 notified the depositary (*i. e.* the addressee of its original Article 124 declaration) of its intention to withdraw from it.[358]

It is somewhat surprising though, that the drafters of Article 15 *bis* (4) 2nd sentence **354** thought it appropriate to choose a slightly different wording as compared to Article 124 (Article 15 *bis*: "[t]he withdrawal of such a declaration may be effected at any time"/"Le retrait d'une telle déclaration peut être effectué à tout moment" – Article 124: "[a] declaration under this article may be withdrawn at any time"/"Il peut à tout moment retirer cette déclaration"). Yet, it still seems that the content of both provisions is nevertheless identical.

Once the period of time for which an opting-out declaration was made under **355** Article 15 *bis* (4) 2nd sentence lapses, the Court may fully exercise its treaty-based, aggression-related jurisdiction even with regard to a crime of aggression arising from an act of aggression committed by the State party that had previously lodged the opting out-declaration.

The wording of Article 15 *bis* (4) 2nd sentence is silent on the question, whether, once **356** an opting-out declaration has been withdrawn, the Court may then retroactively exercise its jurisdiction with regard to a crime of aggression arising from an act of aggression committed by the State party prior to the said withdrawal. Yet, in order to provide for a full *effet utile* of the provision, it seems that the Court would still, *i. e.* even after the opting-out declaration concerning the Court's treaty-based, aggression-related jurisdiction has expired, not be able to exercise its jurisdiction with regard to such a

---

[355] See also McDougall, *The Crime of Aggression under the Rome Statute of the International Criminal Court,* 2013, 267.

[356] For details see Zimmermann, in: Triffterer/Ambos (eds.), *The Rome Statute of the International Criminal Court,* 3rd ed., 2016, Art. 124, mn. 16.

[357] On the withdrawal of declarations made under Article 124 see Zimmermann, in: Triffterer/Ambos (eds.), *The Rome Statute of the International Criminal Court,* 3rd ed., 2016, Art. 124, mn. 9 and 15.

[358] Zimmermann, in: Triffterer/Ambos (eds.), *The Rome Statute of the International Criminal Court,* 3rd ed., 2016, Art. 124, mn. 9.

crime of aggression arising from an act of aggression committed by the State party prior to the withdrawal of the declaration.

357   The last part of the 2nd sentence of Article 15 *bis* (4) contains an obligation of a State party having lodged an opt-out declaration with the Registrar to *bona fide* contemplate ("envisager" in the French text) a withdrawal of such a declaration previously made. Obviously, this does not entail an obligation to actually withdraw any such declaration, and, besides, said obligation only becomes applicable three years after any such declaration has been made. Accordingly, not withdrawing such a declaration does not amount to a violation of the Statute.

358   Unlike Article 124, Article 15 *bis* (4) is not subject to a mandatory reassessment procedure by a review conference.

5. The *de facto* reversal of the opt-out option by Resolution ICC-ASP/ 16/Res.5 (2017)

359   With the activation of the Court's aggression-related jurisdiction on 14 December 2017 by Resolution ICC-ASP/16/Res.5, the ASP effectively reversed the opt-out option of the Kampala amendment.

360   In the preambular part of the said decision, the ASP "recall[ed] resolution RC/Res.6" which had introduced Article 15 *bis* (4) into the Rome Statute. Besides, it also "recall [ed] paragraph 4 of Article 15 *bis* and paragraph 5 of Article 121".[359] Such combined reference might be understood as implying that both provisions are compatible with each other, which would however only be true if the "positive understanding" of Article 121 (5) were the correct interpretation (which is not the case).[360]

361   However, in its operative para. (2), the ASP at the same time continued

> *"that, in accordance with the Rome Statute, the amendments to the Statute regarding the crime of aggression adopted at the Kampala Review Conference enter into force for those States Parties which have accepted the amendments one year after the deposit of their instruments of ratification or acceptance and that in the case of a State referral or* propio motu *investigation the Court shall not exercise its jurisdiction regarding a crime of aggression when committed by a national or on the territory of a State Party that has not ratified or accepted these amendments."*

With this paragraph, the ASP has concluded that Article 121 (5) has to be interpreted in line with the correct, "negative" understanding of that norm. In doing so, the ASP rendered Article 15 *bis* (4) completely redundant, sharing this fate with the one opt-out declaration already lodged thereunder (i.e. the one lodged by Kenya in 2015). While pre-2016, a simultaneous ratification of the Kampala amendments and the deposit of an opting-out declaration might have made sense in order to help reaching the necessary quorum of thirty States under Article 15 *bis* (2) and Article 15 *ter* (2), any such "triggering" effect has now become obsolete once the quorum has been reached.[361]

362   The drafting history of Resolution ICC-ASP/16/Res.5 seems to confirm that the States had indeed wanted to completely set aside any effect of Article 15 *bis* (4), as former drafts had still retained an "opting-out light" approach,[362] stating that the ASP would

---

[359] Resolution ICC-ASP/16/Res.5, 14 December 2017, preambular paras. 1 and 5.
[360] Zimmermann, 16 *JICJ* 2018, 19 (22).
[361] Zimmermann, 16 *JICJ* 2018, 19 (23).
[362] Zimmermann, 16 *JICJ* 2018, 19 (23 *et seq.*).

take note of "the [views] [positions] expressed by States Parties, individually or collectively, as reflected in the Report on the facilitation, or upon adoption of this resolution to be reflected in the Official Records of this session of the Assembly or communicated in writing to the President of the Assembly".[363]

States turned out to be highly divided by this topic. Many of them, Liechtenstein **363** and Switzerland surging ahead, had taken the view that nationals of States which have not ratified the Kampala amendment and who also have not opted out would fall under the Court's jurisdiction if they committed the crime on the territory of a State party that had ratified or accepted the amendment. Another group of States, among them the UK, France, Japan, Canada and Norway, had taken a more restrictive view, arguing that under Article 15 *bis* the Court would not any have jurisdiction over aggression committed by nationals of non-ratifying States or on the territory of such States. After intense negotiations, extending beyond midnight and the date scheduled for completion of the ASP, the ASP's final resolution adopted the latter, restrictive view.[364]

Another result of these tensions was the inclusion of para. (3) of the said Resolution, **364** according to which the ASP "[r]eaffirm[ed] paragraph 1 of Article 40 and paragraph 1 of Article 119 of the Rome Statute in relation to the judicial independence of the judges of the Court". This paragraph reiterates the banality that with regard to any issue arising to the Court's jurisdiction, the matter will be settled by the Court itself without any outside interference.[365]

Only time will tell whether all States parties (also the ones not having been present at **365** that 16th ASP) will accept the understanding as adopted in New York. They also might, the text of Resolution ICC-ASP/16/Res.5 notwithstanding, still submit opting-out declarations in which they might confirm the – in their view – continued relevance of the "positive understanding" of Article 121 (5), and hence the continued necessity to submit opting-out declarations under Article 15 *bis* (4).[366]

Apart from the technical issues on Article 15 *bis*, this "amendment of the amend- **366** ment" raises two main problems. First, it raises serious constitutional concerns for those States which had already ratified the Kampala amendment. Any such domestic ratification law was based on the "positive understanding" of Article 121 (5), as then being reflected in Article 15 *bis* (4). However, Resolution ICC-ASP/16/Res.5 – the *de facto* amendment of the Kampala amendment – was adopted merely by way of a decision of the various State party governments, with immediate effect and without any form of parliamentary approval; though national constitutional law (such as the one of Germany) might set specific limits on the informal development of a treaty regime by the government without a renewed parliamentary approval.[367]

Second, the decision to activate the ICC's jurisdiction on aggression might, in less **367** informed circles, raise high hopes in so far that people will expect the Court to investigate all kinds of aggression although the Court – due to the narrow scope of Article 8 *bis* and now also due to a very limited jurisdiction *ratione personae* – cannot exercise jurisdiction. This might lead to even greater disappointment with the work of the Court.[368]

---

[363] ICC-ASP/16/L.9, ICC-ASP/16/L.9/Rev.1, 13 and 14 December 2017, operative paragraphs 1(a).
[364] Kreß, 16 *JICJ* 2018, 1 (9 *et seq.*).
[365] Zimmermann, 16 *JICJ* 2018, 19 (24).
[366] Zimmermann, 16 *JICJ* 2018, 19 (25).
[367] Zimmermann, 16 *JICJ* 2018, 19 (25 *et seq.*).
[368] Zimmermann, 16 *JICJ* 2018, 19 (28).

6. Interaction with the UN Security Council

368   Under Article 15 *bis* (6)-(9), the Court's exercise of its treaty-based, aggression-related jurisdiction does not depend on a previous determination by the UN Security Council of an act of aggression committed by the State concerned. This constitutes one of the fundamental results reached during the 2010 Review Conference.

369   Article 15 *bis* (6)-(9) lay down, in significant further detail, the various aspects of the relationship between the Court (and mainly the ICC Prosecutor) on the one hand, and the UN Security Council on the other. According to Article 15 *bis* (6), when the ICC Prosecutor wishes to proceed with an investigation in respect of a crime of aggression, he or she shall first ascertain whether the UN Security Council has made such a determination.[369] If it has, the ICC Prosecutor may proceed (para. 7).[370] If the UN Security Council has not made such a determination within six months after the date of notification, further investigations require both, an authorization by the ICC Pre-Trial Division in accordance with the procedure contained in Article 15, and that the UN Security Council has not decided otherwise in accordance with Article 16 (Article 15 *bis* (8)).[371] Finally, Article *15 bis* (9) provides that any finding on the existence of an act of aggression by an organ outside the Court shall not bind the Court.[372]

a) Interaction between the Prosecutor and the UN

Articles 15 *bis* (6) provides as follows:

> *"Where the Prosecutor concludes that there is a reasonable basis to proceed with an investigation in respect of a crime of aggression, he or she shall first ascertain whether the Security Council has made a determination of an act of aggression committed by the State concerned. The Prosecutor shall notify the Secretary-General of the United Nations of the situation before the Court, including any relevant information and documents."*

370   The introductory words of Article 15 *bis* (6) are identical to the ones used in Article 15 (3) except that in the English and French texts the word "if"/"si" (as used in Article 15 (3)) were replaced by the word "where"/"lorsque" in Article 15 *bis* (6), while the Spanish text uses the very same terminology "si" (*i. e.* amounting more to an "if") on both occasions. This leads to the conclusion that there is no difference in meaning. At most, one could say that Article 15 *bis* (6) employs the term "where" in order to express the idea that situations might arise where the Prosecutor concludes that there is a reasonable basis to proceed with an investigation generally, without reaching the same conclusion concerning the crime of aggression. It ought to be noted, however, that there might be also cases in which the ICC Prosecutor concludes that there is a reasonable basis to proceed with an investigation specifically in respect of a crime of aggression, without at the same time reaching the same conclusion as to the other crimes listed in Article 5, and indeed obviously *vice versa*.

371   Given the identical standard used in both Article 15 *bis* (3) and in Article 15 *bis* (6) that there must be a "reasonable basis to proceed with an investigation", the standard

---

[369] For details see *infra* mns. 370 *et seq.*
[370] For details see *infra* mns. 379 *et seq.*
[371] For details see *infra* mns. 381 *et seq.*
[372] For details see *infra* mns. 386 *et seq.*

developed in the Court's jurisprudence as to what is meant by "reasonable basis to proceed" under Article 15 (3)[373] also applies when it comes to Article 15 *bis* (6) with the sole difference that said "reasonable basis" refers to a sub-category of crimes listed in Article 5 only, namely the crime of aggression.

The second part of the first sentence of Article 15 *bis* (6) constitutes the first element **372** in the close interrelationship that the Rome Statute establishes between the Court on the one hand and the UN Security Council on the other. In order to avoid any contradictions between the Court and the UN Security Council to the extent possible and without infringing upon the independence of the Court and its organs, Article 15 *bis* (6) obliges the ICC Prosecutor, before moving ahead with any further steps concerning a possible crime of aggression to *first* clearly establish, as confirmed by the French term "s'assure", whether the Council has not already dealt with the matter and made a determination that an act of aggression has indeed been committed.

Under Article 15 *bis* (6) any such determination can only be made by the UN **373** Security Council as such by way of a resolution adopted under Chapter VII of the Charter. This is due to the fact that the language used in Article 15 *bis* (6), namely the words "determine" and "act of aggression", were taken from Article 39 of the UN Charter. Such a determination cannot thus be made by the President of the UN Security Council by way of a Presidential Statement and even less so by way of a statement by the UN Security Council's President made to the press, the latter being made anyhow not on behalf of the UN Security Council, but rather on behalf of its individual members.[374]

As a matter of practice, the UN Security Council would then normally, provided it **374** ever were to make such a determination, integrate it into the preamble of the respective resolution. Any such determination, to state the obvious, would not however, by the same token, also provide for a referral to the Court under Article 15 *ter*.[375]

In the past, the UN Security Council has only rarely used the term "act of aggres- **375** sion", preferring determinations of threats to the peace. The last time it found that a State had committed an aggressive act was back in 1990 in Resolution 667.[376]

Under Article 15 *bis* (9) any such determination, even when made, would however **376** not be binding upon the Court.[377]

The "State concerned" referred to in (6) is the State committing the alleged "act of **377** aggression" which gives rise to the investigation for the possible commission of a crime of aggression.

Under Article 15 *bis* (6) 2nd sentence, the ICC Prosecutor is under an obligation to **378** keep the UN Secretary-General informed of the situation before the Court and to provide the UN with relevant information and documents concerning possible proceedings. This obligation supplements the more general obligations arising under the Relationship Agreement concluded between the Court and the UN. The obligation enshrined in Article 15 *bis* (6) 2nd sentence is not contained in Article 15 and is thus unique to the crime of aggression, demonstrating the particular relevance of such proceedings for the UN, and, in particular, the UN Security Council. It goes

---

[373] For details see Bergsmo, Pejić and Zhu, in: Triffterer/Ambos (eds.), *The Rome Statute of the International Criminal Court*, 3rd ed., 2016, Art. 15, mns. 20 *et seq.*

[374] Zimmermann, in: Simma *et al.* (eds.), *The Charter of the United Nations. A Commentary*, 3rd ed., 2012, Art. 27, mn. 74.

[375] For further details *infra* mns. 402 *et seq.*

[376] Strapatsas, in: Barriga and Kreß (eds.), *The Crime of Aggression: A Commentary*, 2017, 178 (180); Krisch, in: Simma *et al.* (eds.), *The Charter of the United Nations. A Commentary*, 3rd ed., 2012, Art. 39, mns. 42 *et seq.*

[377] For details *see infra* mns. 386 *et seq.*

without saying that any such information received by the UN Secretary-General would then, as a matter of course, be forwarded to the UN Security Council, given that the main purpose of this information is to trigger the 6-month period provided for in article 15 *bis* (8) to commence and, by the same token, to provide the Security Council with a 6-month period to consider whether to make use of its powers under Article 16.[378]

b) UN Security Council determinations of an act of aggression

379 Once the UN Security Council has made a determination within the meaning of Article 15 *bis* (6),[379] the ICC Prosecutor may then proceed with a full investigation pursuant to Articles 53 and 54 in respect of a crime of aggression (rather than a mere preliminary examination), thus moving from the proceedings governed by Article 15 into the realm of Article 53 and other provisions in Part 5 of the Statute,[380] without the need of a formal UN Security Council or State referral.

380 It is indeed worth noting that, unlike in the case of possible investigations concerning other crimes listed in Article 5, a State referral is of no relevance when it comes to investigating a crime of aggression. In case a situation is referred to the ICC Prosecutor by a State, possibly involving both crimes under Article 5 (a)-(c) and the crime of aggression, the Prosecutor would thus be in a position to immediately start investigations with regard to the former, but would have to wait for six months before doing so with respect to the alleged crime of aggression. Even then, the Prosecutor would eventually have to seek authorization by the ICC Pre-Trial Division under Article 15 *bis* (8), provided that no relevant determination by the Security Council is forthcoming.[381]

c) Lack of a determination by the UN Security Council, and the role of the Pre-Trial Division

381 Article 15 *bis* (8) addresses the situation in which the UN Security Council, after having been informed via the UN Secretary-General of a pending preliminary investigation concerning a possible crime of aggression, does not make a finding of an act of aggression, as outlined above[382], within the prescribed six-month period either because the UN Security Council simply remains silent on the matter, or because a draft resolution that would have made such a determination has failed to garner the necessary majority, as required by Article 27 of the UN Charter.[383]

382 The six-month period contemplated in Article 15 *bis* (8) begins, as the text puts it, with "the date of notification", *i.e.* at the point in time at which the UN Secretary-General has been informed by the ICC Prosecutor pursuant to Article 15 *bis* (6) 2nd sentence.[384]

383 In case the UN Security Council fails to make a determination within the meaning of Article 15 *bis* (7)[385] (or indeed even determines that no act of aggression has been committed in a given case), Article 15 *bis* (8) provides for an alternative, namely that

---

[378] See *supra* mns. 381 *et seq.*

[379] See *supra* mns. 370 *et seq.*

[380] See *mutatis mutandis* Bergsmo, Pejić and Zhu, in: Triffterer/Ambos (eds.), *The Rome Statute of the International Criminal Court*, 3rd ed., 2016, Art. 15, mn. 21.

[381] See *supra* mns. 381 *et seq.*

[382] See *supra* mn. 370.

[383] As to the voting requirements under Article 27 UN Charter, see Zimmermann, in: Simma *et al.* (eds.), *The Charter of the United Nations*, 3rd ed., 2012, Art. 27, *passim*.

[384] For details see *supra* mn. 378.

[385] See *supra* mns. 381 *et seq.*

the ICC Prosecutor, seeking to act *proprio motu*, must then seek permission by the ICC Pre-Trial Division.

As the text itself confirms by making reference to the procedure contained in Article 15, the procedure is *mutatis mutandis* identical to the one provided for in the said provision as far as the other crimes listed in Article 5 are concerned.[386] The sole, yet important, difference lies in the fact that while Article 15 (3) and (4) provide for an authorization by a ICC Pre-Trial Chamber (as opposed to "Division") consisting of three judges (Article 39 (2)(b)(iii)), Article 15 *bis* (8) requires an authorization by the ICC Pre-Trial Division consisting of no less than six judges (Article 39 (1) 2nd sentence), which confirms the relevance and political sensitivity of the decision to eventually enable such an investigation to go forward.   **384**

This part of Article 15 *bis* (8) confirms in a declaratory manner the prerogatives of the UN Security Council provided for in Article 16.[387] Accordingly, the UN Security Council, acting under Chapter VII of the UN Charter, may also request the Court not to commence or proceed with an investigation or prosecution for a (renewable) period of twelve months with respect to an alleged crime of aggression. It seems, however, given the placement and the context of the provision as forming part of Article 15 *bis*, Article 15 *bis* (8) enables the UN Security Council to "tailor" its request under Article 16 to exclusively concern the crime of aggression. Put otherwise, it seems that the UN Security Council might prevent, for a renewable period of twelve months, the Court from investigating the crime of aggression, while at the same time letting the Court consider the very same facts concerning possible violations of the *jus in bello*, acts of genocide or crimes against humanity.   **385**

d) Independence of the Court

Article 15 *bis* (9) confirms that the Court, when asked to make a finding on a crime of aggression, which under Article 8 *bis* presupposes that an act of aggression has been committed for which a State then incurs State responsibility, is not bound by a finding made by an institution which does not form part of the Court. A literal reading of the wording seems to imply that the Court would not be bound by a positive determination that an act of aggression has occurred only. This is due to the fact that Article 15 *bis* (9) refers to "[a] determination of an act of aggression" rather than stating that a determination on an act of aggression by an organ outside the Court would be without prejudice to the Court's own findings under this Statute. On the other hand, para. (9) of Article 15 *bis*, in its English version, does *not* make use of the definite article "the",[388] which would have further reinforced this limited understanding of para. (9) as applying to positive determinations only as being not binding for the Court. At the same time, the French text does just this when referring to "*[l]e* constat d'un acte d'agression" rather than referring to "*un* constat d'un acte d'agression". This is further confirmed by the Spanish version ("La determinación de que *hubo* acto de agresión"), which by using a past tense defines a determination in terms of Article 15 *bis* (9) as the positive assertion that an act of aggression has occurred.   **386**

It seems, however, that an interpretation in line with the provision's object and purpose, namely to safeguard the judicial integrity and independence of the Court,   **387**

---

[386] For details on Article 15 see Bergsmo, Pejić and Zhu, in: Triffterer/Ambos (eds.), *The Rome Statute of the International Criminal Court*, 3rd ed., 2016, Art. 15, *passim*.

[387] See Bergsmo, Pejić and Zhu, in: Triffterer/Ambos (eds.), *The Rome Statute of the International Criminal Court*, 3rd ed., 2016, Art. 16, *passim*.

[388] Article 15 *bis* (9) would have thus read: "*The* determination of an act of aggression by an organ outside the Court shall be without prejudice to the Court's own findings under this Statute."

invites a broader interpretation. It follows that *any* form of determination relating to an act of aggression, whether a positive or a negative one (for example one stating that a State allegedly having committed an act of aggression had instead acted in the exercise of its right under Article 51 of the UN Charter), cannot therefore have an impact on the Court's ability to independently make a determination concerning the act of aggression that has possibly led to the commission of a crime of aggression. As a matter of fact, were it otherwise and would accordingly an *argumentum e contrario* apply, the reference to Article 16 in Article 15 *bis* (8) would be partially redundant, since any negative determination that no act of aggression has occurred would then at least *de facto* bar the Court from exercising its jurisdiction in a meaningful manner, without the need for the UN Security Council to make use of its Article 16 powers.

388 During the negotiations leading to the adoption of the Kampala amendments on the crime of aggression, it was the independence of the Court *vis-à-vis* the Security Council that formed the core of the debate. The reference in the text to any "organ outside the Court", the findings of which shall not prejudice to the Court's own findings under this Statute, is however broader. Accordingly, Article 15 *bis* (9) does not apply only to determinations by the UN Security Council as to the existence or non-existence of an act of aggression, but also to judicial findings made for purposes of State responsibility *e.g.* by the ICJ, or by arbitral tribunals such as the Ethiopian-Eritrean Claims Commission. In line with the jurisprudence of the ICJ,[389] the underlying judicial philosophy of which applies *mutatis mutandis*, the Court should however, in principle, accept as highly persuasive relevant findings made by other judicial bodies that have dealt with the underlying act of aggression.

389 Finally, the last words of Article 15 *bis* (9) ("the Court's own findings *under this Statute*") are in line with the first sentence of Understanding no. 4, namely that any findings by the Court on the commission on a crime of aggression are not supposed to have a bearing on the general concept of the prohibition of the use of force under general international law.[390]

7. Issues of jurisdiction

a) Exercise of jurisdiction

390 Setting out the parameters of the exercise by the Court of its treaty-based, aggression-related jurisdiction, Article 15 *bis* contains manifold deviations from Article 12, 13 and 15. In order to avoid these peculiarities to have any impact on the exercise of the Court's jurisdiction with respect to the other crimes referred to in Article 5, namely genocide, crimes against humanity and war crimes, Article 15 *bis* (10) specifies that the Court's exercise of its jurisdiction remains unaffected. This, however, may lead to practical hurdles, for example, when nationals of various States are suspects in the same proceedings involving both violations of the *jus ad bellum*, as well as possibly also acts of genocide, crimes against humanity and war crimes. In such a scenario a split jurisdictional regime might apply. This would depend on whether certain suspects might also be prosecuted for having committed the crime of aggression or rather not, because their home State is either not a contracting party of the Statute or

---

[389] *ICJ, Application of the Convention on the Prevention and Punishment of the Crime of Genocide (Croatia v. Serbia)*, Judgment (Merits), ICJ Rep. 2015, para. 182; see also *ICJ, Application of the Convention on the Prevention and Punishment of the Crime of Genocide (Bosnia and Herzegovina v. Serbia and Montenegro)*, Judgment (Merits), ICJ Rep. 2007, 43, 134, para. 223.

[390] See *supra* mn. 203.

because, while being a State party, it is not subject to the Court's aggression-related jurisdiction.

b) Exclusion of jurisdiction concerning non-parties

Article 15 *bis* (5), the relevant wording of which is *mutatis mutandis* identical to **391** Article 121 (5), provides that in respect of a State that is not a party to the Rome Statute, the Court shall not exercise its jurisdiction when the crime of aggression was committed by that State's nationals or on its territory. Article 15 *bis* (5) thus derogates, when it comes to the crime of aggression, from the Court's general jurisdictional set-up provided for in Article 12, under which even crimes committed by nationals of a State that is not a contracting party come within the Court's jurisdiction, provided they are committed on the territory of a contracting State.

The first part of Article 15 *bis* (5) clarifies that it only deals with the legal situation of **392** States that are not parties to the Statute at the relevant time, while the legal situation of States that are parties to the Statute, but have not ratified or accepted the Kampala amendment on the crime of aggression, is governed by Article 15 *bis* (4) (though Article 15 *bis* (4) has effectively been rendered completely redundant by ASP Resolution ICC-ASP/16/Res.5[391]).[392]

Article 15 *bis* (5) applies to proceedings both, directed against nationals of a State not **393** a party to the Statute and related to a crime of aggression committed on the territory of such a State, even when committed by a national of a State party and committed against such a non-State party.

One might argue though that properly understood, Article 15 *bis* (5) was meant to **394** leave the option open for the Court to exercise jurisdiction where either nationals of a State not a party to the Statute commit a crime of aggression on the territory of a State party, or where nationals of a State party commit the crime of aggression on the territory of a third State not a State party of the Statute, *i. e.* where an alternative jurisdictional link exists. In line with the debate surrounding the proper understanding of Article 121 (5), this is commonly referred to as the so-called "positive understanding" of Article 15 *bis* (5).[393] Such an understanding is refuted, however, if there is need, by the equally authentic French texts of both, Article 15 *bis* (5) and Article 121 (5), which clarify that the phrase is intended to provide for a full exclusion of jurisdiction *vis-à-vis* the State party that does not accept the amendment,[394] given that the French version of Article 15 *bis* (5) provides that "[l]a Cour *n'exerce pas sa compétence* à l'égard du crime d'agression quand celui-ci est commis par des ressortissants de cet État ou sur son territoire".[395] This stands in contrast to the wording of Article 124, the wording of which foresees that the State making the declaration under Article 124 "does not accept the jurisdiction of the Court". Yet, even this latter formula is understood in light of its object and purpose as barring the Court's war crime-related jurisdiction *in toto vis-à-vis* the State that has made a declaration under Article 124, even if otherwise a jurisdictional link were to exist ('negative' understanding of Article 124).[396]*A fortiori* such a

---

[391] See *supra* at mns. 359 *et seq.*

[392] For details see *supra* mn. 327 *et seq.*

[393] With respect to Article 121 (5): Reisinger Coracini, 21 *LeidenJIL* 2008, 699 (707).

[394] Zimmermann, 10 *JICJ* 2012, 209 (217); see also McDougall, *The Crime of Aggression under the Rome Statute of the International Criminal Court,* 2013, 256.

[395] Article 121 (5) in turn reads: "La Cour n'exerce pas sa compétence à l'égard d'un crime faisant l'objet de cet amendement lorsque ce crime a été commis par un ressortissant d'un État Partie qui n'a pas accepté l'amendement ou sur le territoire de cet État"; emphasis added.

[396] See Zimmermann, in: Triffterer/Ambos (eds.), *The Rome Statute of the International Criminal Court*, 3rd ed., 2016, Art. 124, mn. 14.

negative understanding must then also apply to Article 15 *bis* (5). Accordingly, the Court may, under no circumstances (apart from Article 15 *ter*), exercise its jurisdiction with regard to a given crime that has been committed by nationals of a non-ratifying State party or on its territory, even if the Court would otherwise enjoy jurisdiction on the basis of the crime being committed on the territory or by the nationals of another contracting party.[397] This leads to the somewhat counter-intuitive result that even where a State, not party to the Statute, is the victim of the underlying act of aggression committed by nationals of a State that has fully accepted the Court's treaty-based, aggression-related jurisdiction, the Court cannot exercise such jurisdiction, subject however to a declaration made by the respective third State under Article 12 (3), accepting the Court's jurisdiction *ad hoc*.[398]

c) Domestic jurisdiction over the crime of aggression

395 Understanding no. 5 adopted at the Kampala conference[399] provides:

> *"It is understood that the amendments shall not be interpreted as creating the right or obligation to exercise domestic jurisdiction with respect to an act of aggression committed by another State."*

396 It thereby confirms in a declaratory manner that the inclusion of the amendments on the crime of aggression in the Statute has no bearing on the exercise of domestic jurisdiction over the crime of aggression, either by way of obliging a State to do so or by implying a parallel right. It is noteworthy however that the said Understanding refers solely to the exercise of domestic jurisdiction with respect to an act of aggression committed by another State. This might be perceived as implying *e contrario* that, when it comes to the exercise of domestic jurisdiction with respect to an act of aggression committed by the forum State, the amendments might have created such an obligation, while a right to do so exists as a matter of course anyhow. Yet, under the principle of complementarity a State is not obliged to exercise criminal jurisdiction over its own nationals, the sole consequence of a non-exercise of domestic jurisdiction with respect to an alleged crime of aggression being that the Court would then be in a position to do so, provided it has jurisdiction.

8. Outlook

397 Article 15 *bis* was finally adopted by the ASP with a large degree of controversy. Whereas the ASP was able to finally agree on the inclusion of the definition by Article 8 *bis*, Article 15 *bis* created significant challenges to the Court's possibility of exercising jurisdiction over the crime in the future.

398 Nevertheless, Article 15 *bis* covers the exercise of jurisdiction over the crime of aggression through State referrals and the *propriu motu* powers of the ICC Prosecutor. On 14 December 2017, this jurisdiction has been activated by the ASP.

399 Yet the biggest challenge will continue to come with respect to the opt-out mechanism. While Resolution ICC-ASP/16/Res.5 of 14 December 2017 rendered Article 15 *bis*

---

[397] Werle and Jessberger, *Principles of International Criminal Law*, 3rd ed., 2014, 554; Schmalenbach, *JZ* 2010, 745 (749); *cf.* Ambos, 53 *GYbIL* 2010, 463 (506); see also the statement by Japan, RC/11, Annex VII, at 121, criticizing that "[...] the new Article 15 *bis* 1 *quarter* [now Article 15 *bis* (5)] [...] solidifies a blanket and automatic impunity of nationals of non-State Parties [...]".

[398] See *supra* mn. 335.

[399] As to the normative relevance of those understandings see Heller, 10 *JICJ* 2012, 229.

(4) completely redundant, only time will show whether all States parties accept such an understanding or whether they will continue to lodge opt-out declarations.

On the other hand, the amendments provided a very important role in terms of the **400** relationship with the UN Security Council, although the Court will not be dependent on any determination – or lack therefore – on the commission of an act of aggression by the UN Security Council.

Most importantly, it builds upon the role of States in referring a situation of **401** aggression by way of State referrals, as well as on the role of the Prosecutor to investigate and prosecute through his/her own powers.

V.
UN SECURITY COUNCIL-BASED JURISDICTION
(ARTICLE 15 *TER* ROME STATUTE)

Article 15 *ter* – "[e]xercise of jurisdiction over the crime of aggression (Security **402** Council referral)" – exclusively deals with referrals by the UN Security Council, while State referrals as well as proceedings started *proprio motu* by the Prosecutor are addressed in turn, as far as the crime of aggression is concerned, by Article 15 *bis*. Of the three different ways of triggering the Court's jurisdiction established under Article 13, Article 15 *ter* – as introduced into the Rome Statute as part of the Kampala compromise on the crime of aggression along Article 15 *bis* and 8 *bis* – relates to Article 13 (b). Article 13 (b) provides that "[a] situation in which one or more of such crimes appears to have been committed is referred to the Prosecutor by the Security Council acting under Chapter VII of the Charter of the United Nations".

While Article 15 *bis* contains significant deviations from the regular jurisdictional **403** scheme underlying the Rome Statute, Article 15 *ter* is much more in line with the scheme otherwise applying in case of UN Security Council referrals, as provided for in Article 13 (b). Not the least, this holds true for the fact that in case of a UN Security Council referral, as opposed to when the Court exercises its treaty-based aggression-related jurisdiction,[400] the Court might even, as confirmed by Understanding no. 2 of the Review Conference, be able to exercise its aggression-related jurisdiction when respective crimes of aggression were committed on the territory of a State not having accepted the Court's aggression-related jurisdiction, or by nationals of such a State.[401]

As has been shown,[402] the content of Article 15 *bis*, and in particular the question **404** whether the Court should be in a position to exercise its treaty-based jurisdiction concerning the crime of aggression regardless of whether the UN Security Council had previously made a determination as to the occurrence of an act of aggression or not, constituted one of the most vividly debated issues prior to and during the 2010 Kampala Review Conference. In contrast thereto, during the negotiation process there existed, by and large, a consensus that *mutatis mutandis* the jurisdictional scheme underlying Article 13 (b) should also apply when it comes to the crime of aggression alongside the eventual exercise, by the Court, of its treaty-based, aggression-related jurisdiction.

From early on, the SWGCA agreed in principle that a UN Security Council referral **405** should not depend on whether the respective States had ratified the amendments,[403] an assumption not challenged during the 2010 Review Conference. However, during the Review Conference, the participants discussed (initiated by a proposal by Argentina, Brazil and Switzerland) whether UN Security Council referrals should be possible after a single ratification of the amendments, in accordance with Article 121 (5) of the Rome Statute (covering amendments to Articles 5–8 of the Rome Statute). Though this idea has not been adopted eventually, the respective proposal floored by Argentine, Brazil and Switzerland built towards the momentum triggering the introduction of a separate Article 15 *ter*. A further proposal by these States (handed in together with Canada on

---

[400] For details see *supra* mns. 391 *et seq*.
[401] For details see *infra* mn. 405.
[402] See *supra* mn. 276.
[403] Barriga, in: Barriga and Kreß (eds.), *The Travaux Préparatoires of the Crime of Aggression*, 2012, 3 (40).

9 June 2010) featured a consent-based jurisdiction regime, including an opt-out option, and a non-exclusive UN Security Council filter,[404] and constituted the basis for the final drafting process.

1. Exercise of jurisdiction

Article 15 *ter* (1) provides:

> *"The Court may exercise jurisdiction over the crime of aggression in accordance with Article 13, paragraph (b), subject to the provisions of this article."*

406   Given that Article 15 *ter* (1) is, *mutatis mutandis*, identical to Article 15 *bis* (1), the very same considerations which apply to Article 15 *bis* (1) as outlined above,[405] also apply with regard to Article 15 *ter* (1). This is in reference to the Court's ability to exercise jurisdiction over the crime of aggression. It is with the obvious exception that the last part of Article 15 *ter* (1) makes reference to Article 13 (b), rather than to lit (a) and (c). Thus, where Article 13 (b) denotes those situations where the UN Security Council, acting under Chapter VII of the UN Charter, refers a particular situation to the ICC Prosecutor, Article 13 (a) and (c) covers State party referrals as well as the *proprio motu* powers of the ICC Prosecutor, respectively.

407   In line with the compromise reached during the 2010 Kampala Review Conference, Article 15 *ter* (1) provides that "[t]he Court may exercise jurisdiction over the crime of aggression in accordance with Article 13, paragraph (b)".[406] Article 15 *ter* thus exclusively covers UN Security Council referrals, whereas State referrals and proceedings initiated *proprio motu* by the Prosecutor are regulated by Article 15 *bis* (1).[407]

408   Such Security Council referrals are then governed by the regular requirements contained in Article 13 (b), namely that the situation has been referred to the ICC Prosecutor by the UN Security Council acting under Chapter VII of the UN Charter.[408]

409   As already indicated by the very term itself, any such "referral" by the UN Security Council does not require an explicit previous determination of an act of aggression, nor would such a referral amount to one, even less so since the Security Council rarely ever makes such specific determinations.[409] What is more, one might even wonder whether the UN Security Council has to formally act under Chapter VII, or whether instead a reference to Chapter VII might be implied in any such referral to the ICC Prosecutor.[410]

410   In contrast to Article 15 *bis* (4), Article 15 *ter* does not provide for the possibility of a State's opting out of the Court's aggression-related UN Security Council-based jurisdiction (though, given the decision made by Resolution ICC-ASP/16/Res.5 in 2017, Article 15 *bis* (4) has *de facto* been rescinded[411]). The Court may thus exercise its jurisdiction under Article 15 *ter* regardless of whether a State party is subject to the

---

[404] Barriga, in: Barriga and Kreß (eds.), *The Travaux Préparatoires of the Crime of Aggression,* 2012, 3 (49, 51); also see Ambos, *Treatise on International Criminal Law, Volume II,* 2014, 192 *et seq.*

[405] See *supra* mns. 279 *et seq.*

[406] As to the specific content of Article 13 (a) and (c) see Schabas and Pecorella, in: Triffterer/Ambos (eds.), *The Rome Statute of the International Criminal Court,* 3rd ed., 2016, Art. 13, mn. 15 and 20 respectively.

[407] See mns. 279 *et seq.*

[408] For further details see Schabas and Pecorella, in: Triffterer/Ambos (eds.), *The Rome Statute of the International Criminal Court,* 3rd ed., 2016, Art. 13, mns. 16 *et seq.*

[409] See already mn. 375.

[410] As to the question whether the Security Council may implicitly act under Chapter VII, without formally invoking its Chapter VII powers see generally Zimmermann, *Israeli Law Review* 2016, 1 *et seq.*

[411] See *supra* at mns. 359 *et seq.*

Court's treaty-based aggression-related jurisdiction under Article 15 *bis* or whether it is not a State party at all. This is confirmed by Understanding no. 2 which provides:

> *"It is understood that the Court shall exercise jurisdiction over the crime of aggression on the basis of a Security Council referral in accordance with Article 13, paragraph (b), of the Statute irrespective of whether the State concerned has accepted the Court's jurisdiction in this regard."*

Article 15 *ter* (1) further clarifies that, while acknowledging the possibility of UN Security Council referrals under Article 13 (a) even when it comes to the crime of aggression, such proceedings are then subject to the specific requirements and conditions contained in Article 15 *ter* (2)–(5), as constituting *lex specialis*. **411**

One issue however not addressed as such in Article 15 *ter* is whether the UN Security Council may, when referring a situation under Article 13 (b) in conjunction with Article 15 *ter* (1), either make a selective referral by only referring the crime of aggression, or, on the contrary, while referring a situation as such, could by the same token refrain from also endowing the Court with a UN Security Council-based aggression-related jurisdiction. Yet, given that under Article 13 (b), the UN Security Council refers "a situation" rather than a specific crime,[412] and further given that Article 15 *ter* (1) makes reference to the Court, exercising its jurisdiction "in accordance with Article 13, paragraph (b)" in case of a UN Security Council referral potentially involving the commission of the crime of aggression, it seems that the UN Security Council is faced with an either/or-situation. On the one hand, it can refer a situation as such, thereby enabling the Court to also exercise substance-matter jurisdiction *vis-à-vis* the crime of aggression; on the other hand, it cannot refer such a situation at all, thereby preventing the Court from prosecuting any of the other crimes listed in Article 5, unless the Court could exercise its treaty-based jurisdiction over those crimes, but had no jurisdiction over the crime of aggression, given the jurisdictional limitations contained in Article 15 *bis* (4) and (5).[413] **412**

One might also assume, however, that as a third alternative the UN Security Council could *de facto* limit the Court's substance-matter jurisdiction by deliberately circumscribing the Court's temporal jurisdiction in a specific manner. The UN Security Council could thus refer a "situation" covering only a limited period of time (*e.g.* "the situation in State x from date y to date z"), thereby enabling investigations only with regard to the alleged crimes having taken place during that specific period, such as the initial crime of aggression, without providing the Court with jurisdiction over *e.g.* war crimes, which might have taken place only after that date, or indeed *vice versa*. **413**

With regard to the question of whether the UN Security Council might circumscribe the individuals who shall face prosecution, States as well as the Court seem to have accepted a division of roles between the UN Security Council and the Prosecutor,[414] **414**

---

[412] Apart from the wording of Article 13, this is also confirmed by Article 44 (2) Rules of Procedure and Evidence. While this provision relates to Article 12 (3) of the Statute, it underscores that even where the Statute (mistakenly) refers to the acceptance, by a State, of the Court's jurisdiction with respect to a "crime in question", any such acceptance relates to an overall situation rather than a specific crime; for further details see Schabas and Pecorella, in: Triffterer/Ambos (eds.), *The Rome Statute of the International Criminal Court*, 3rd ed., 2016, Art. 13, mns. 15 *et seq.* with further references.

[413] See Schmalenbach, *JZ* 2010, 745 (751).

[414] McDougall, *The Crime of Aggression under the Rome Statute of the International Criminal Court*, 2013, 276 *et seq.*; For the opposing view, see Condorelli and Villalpando, in: Cassese (ed.), *The Rome Statute of the International Criminal Court: A Commentary, Volume II*, 2002, 627 (633), who argue that the Security Council may limit the referral of a situation to certain individuals, but that such a limitation does not prevent the Prosecutor from stopping to proceed on these grounds or from initiating further investigations.

given that UN Security Council Resolution 1593 (2005)[415] as well as UN Security Council Resolution 1970 (2011),[416] have both specifically excluded certain groups of individuals from the Court's jurisdiction. However, when it comes to limiting a "situation" not by way of defining the individuals coming within the Court's jurisdiction *ratione personae*, but by way of only referring a certain period of time, such a limitation would still comply with the UN Security Council's position towards the Court, as the Council would not try to act as a Prosecutor, who has to select individual defendants when assessing the results of his own investigations. Rather, the UN Security Council would merely make use of its prerogatives under Chapter VII of the Charter, in order to assess which factual situations (and if so within what limits) constitute a threat to international peace and security in accordance with Article 39 of the UN Charter.

415   It is also worth noting that where the Court is in a position to exercise its treaty-based jurisdiction over the crimes listed in Article 5 (1) (a)-(c), but not its treaty-based jurisdiction related to the crime of aggression due to the jurisdictional aggression-specific limitations contained in Article 15 *bis* (4) and (5), a UN Security Council referral under Article 13 (b) (in conjunction with Article 15 *ter* (1)) would *de facto* amount to such a partial referral.

2. Entry into force and jurisdiction *ratione temporis* over the crime of aggression

Article 15 *ter* (2) and (3) respectively provide:

> *"The Court may exercise jurisdiction only with respect to crimes of aggression committed one year after the ratification or acceptance of the amendments by thirty States Parties.*
>
> *The Court shall exercise jurisdiction over the crime of aggression in accordance with this article, subject to a decision to be taken after 1 January 2017 by the same majority of States Parties as is required for the adoption of an amendment to the Statute."*

416   Article 15 *ter* (2) and (3), as well as Understanding no. 1, are thus *mutatis mutandis* identical to Article 15 *bis* (2) and (3) respectively except that Understanding no. 1 refers to "a decision in accordance with Article 15 *ter*, paragraph 3", while Understanding no. 3 refers to such a decision taken "in accordance with Article 15 *bis*, paragraph 3". These two specific paragraphs refer to the Court's ability to exercise its jurisdiction one year after the ratification or acceptance of the amendments and after a decision made by the States parties (as taken place on 14 December 2017, activating the Court's jurisdiction as of 17 July 2018). Accordingly, the same considerations that apply to those latter provisions[417] also apply to the former.

3. Independence of the Court

Article 15 (4) provides:

> *"A determination of an act of aggression by an organ outside the Court shall be without prejudice to the Court's own findings under this Statute."*

---

[415] UN DOC S/RES/1593, 31 March 2005, Situation in Darfur, para. 6.
[416] UN DOC S/RES/1970, 26 February 2011, Situation in Libya, para. 6.
[417] See mns. 286 *et seq.*

Article 15 *ter* (4), referring to the non-prejudicial nature of a determination of an act **417**
of aggression by a non-ICC organ, is completely identical to Article 15 *bis* (9).
Accordingly, the same considerations applying to this latter provision[418] also apply to
the former. It is worth noting, however, that even a referral by the UN Security Council
under Chapter VII in conjunction with Article 13 (b) and Article 15 *ter* (1) does not
necessarily *per se* amount to such a determination. This is due to the fact that Article 39
of the UN Charter does not require an act of aggression to have taken place in order to
trigger the Security Council's Chapter VII powers.[419] Accordingly, and as a whole, even
once the UN Security Council has referred a situation to the Court, the latter remains
independent and may deviate from the findings of the UN Security Council.[420]

4. Relationship with jurisdiction over other crimes

Finally, Article 15 *ter* (5), on the non-prejudicial nature of this provision with respect **418**
to other jurisdictional provisions related to the other crimes, is completely identical to
Article 15 *bis* (10). Accordingly, the same considerations which apply to this latter
provision[421] also apply to the former.

5. Outlook

Article 15 *ter* found a balance between competing State interests on the role of the **419**
UN Security Council as having the primary responsibility for the maintenance of
international peace and security, while also ensuring the independence of the Court.
The most important aspect of the inclusion of Article 15 *ter* ensures that the Court is
not dependant on the UN Security Council to make a determination as to whether or
not an act of aggression has been committed. This is especially important given the
politicized nature of the UN Security Council, especially on issues as divisive as
aggression.

Yet given the history of the UN Security Council in failing to ever make a **420**
determination of an act of aggression, it remains to be seen as to what extent it may
make a referral for the purposes of investigations and prosecutions.

---

[418] See mns. 386 *et seq.*

[419] Krisch, in: Simma *et al.* (eds.), *The Charter of the United Nations. A Commentary*, 3rd ed., 2012,
Art. 39, mns. 13, 45 *et seq.*

[420] Clark, 2 *GoJIL* 2010, 689 (703); Reisinger Coracini, 2 *GoJIL* 2010, 745 (749); Werle and Jessberger,
Principles of International Criminal Law, 3rd ed., 2014, 553; for a view with a differing emphasis see
McDougall, *The Crime of Aggression under the Rome Statute of the International Criminal Court*, 2013,
278, who stresses that "this paragraph should not be taken to mean that Security Council resolutions
determining that an act of aggression has occurred will be of no material effect in the Court reaching its
own conclusion as to whether the definition of an act of aggression under Article 8 *bis* (2), or indeed the
crime of aggression under Article 8 *bis* (1), has been met".

[421] See mn. 390.

VI.
SUMMARY AND OUTLOOK: CRIME OF AGGRESSION
AND THE ICC POST-2018

It took a considerable amount of time and effort to finally include the crime of aggression **421** within the Court's jurisdiction. This discussion shifted between a significant number of fora, before finding its way to the 2010 Kampala Review Conference in Kampala. While the definition of the crime of aggression and the role of the UN Security Council were both key divisive issues for States, it was the latter that took until the very last minute to resolve. The result was the crime of aggression's inclusion in Article 8 *bis* covering the definition, with the additions of Article 15 *bis* covering State referrals and the *proprio motu* powers of the ICC Prosecutor, and Article 15 *ter* covering UN Security Council referrals.

Article 8 *bis* included within it the definition of what constitutes a crime of aggression, **422** being a manifest violation of the UN Charter. The most interesting aspect of the inclusion of Article 8 *bis* was that the definition had been for years a divisive issue with many States not recognizing the customary status of the definition and the acts as contained in UN General Assembly Resolution 3314. In the end, Article 8 *bis* borrowed the language of the UN Charter, the UN General Assembly's *Friendly Relations Declaration* and – primarily – Resolution 3314, to define what constitutes an act of aggression.

Article 15 *bis* encompasses State referrals and *proprio motu* powers of the ICC **423** Prosecutor concerning the crime of aggression. Its provisions cover first and foremost, the temporal jurisdiction of the Court. This means that the Court can only exercise its jurisdiction one year after the ratification or acceptance of the amendments by thirty States parties. Further, it must be adopted by the necessary majority of the ASP after 1 January 2017, this decision now having taken place on 14 December 2017, activating the Court's jurisdiction over the crime of aggression as of 17 July 2018. Article 15 *bis* also covers the relationship between the ICC Prosecutor and the UN, primarily the UN Security Council. This includes the independence of the Court in investigating and prosecuting the crime of aggression.

Within Article 15 *bis,* where a State referral is made or where the ICC Prosecutor **424** exercises her or his *propriu motu* powers, and where the ICC Prosecutor concludes that there is a reasonable basis to proceed with an investigation, the Prosecutor must ascertain as to whether the UN Security Council has made a determination of an act of aggression. The Prosecutor is required to notify the UN Secretary-General of the situation and submit any relevant information and documentation pertaining to the situation. If the UN Security Council makes a determination on an act of aggression, the Prosecutor would then be able to proceed with an investigation. If, within 6 months, no such determination is made, the Prosecutor may then request authorization for an investigation from the Pre-Trial Chamber in accordance with the relevant provisions of the Rome Statute.

Article 15 *ter* in turn regulates the exercise of jurisdiction of the crime of the **425** aggression through UN Security Council referrals. It only covers *ratione temporis* crimes of aggression committed one year after the ratification or acceptance of the amendments by thirty States parties and after the jurisdiction has been activated by the ASP.

One might wonder whether adding the crime of aggression might not overburden the **426** Court, in terms of the time, resources and finances required. During times where the Court has to deal with significant challenges, including increased preliminary examinations, investigations and cases, there has been pressure to ensure zero-growth of the

Court's budget. It is not unlikely that a State contributing towards the Court's budget will use it as a means to decrease the Court's influence, particularly where it may involve investigations and prosecutions against itself, or against an allied State. It is only more likely, that if a situation occurs in the future with respect to the crime of aggression, States may use and continue to use the Court's budget as a means of limiting its reach.

427   However, due to the concrete limits that Resolution ICC-ASP/16/Res.5 brought to the jurisdiction *ratione personae* by reversing the amendment's opt-out procedure (combined with a very limited material definition of aggression contained in Article 8 *bis*, which leaves little room for its application), now one might wonder whether maybe the actual threat is rather an "underburdening" of the Court. Now (a referral by the Security Council under article 15 *ter* set aside) only acts of aggression involving, on both sides of the armed conflict, two of the currently 37 States that have ratified the Kampala amendment would come within the jurisdiction of the Court. A look at the list of those States, including Andorra, Austria, Costa Rica, Lichtenstein, Luxembourg, Malta, Samoa, San Marino, Switzerland or Trinidad and Tobago, confirms that it is unlikely that the Court will in the foreseeable future be faced with any situation in which its treaty-based aggression-related jurisdiction will become relevant.[422]

428   Now that the Court's aggression-related jurisdiction has been activated as of 17 July 2018, it remains to be seen how far the Court will eventually progress in terms of investigating and prosecuting the crime of aggression.

429   The UN Security Council's willingness to refer a situation to the ICC Prosecutor is also questionable. First, it has a severely limited "jurisprudence" on aggression. Second, three of the permanent five members of the Council (China, Russia and the United States) have neither joined the Rome Statute of 1998, nor have they even less obviously accepted the Kampala amendments. Besides, the two other permanent members of the Security Council, i.e. France and the United Kingdom have been in the forefront of limiting the Court's treaty-based aggression-related jurisdiction. Of course, politically-speaking, this would not only be a challenge in terms of those States themselves, but of States that may be considered as their allies, should such an initiative be tabled before the Security Council. Its members will continue to protect themselves and their allies against any attempts to refer a situation to the ICC Prosecutor; and especially those three that are not States parties to the Rome Statute will still continue to wield a considerable amount of influence to limit the Court's reach. The UN Security Council has failed to significantly move against aggression in the past and has done much to ensure that no other mechanism, including the UN General Assembly, can move forward in dealing with acts. From their perspective, the crime of aggression should remain within the domain of the Security Council as having the primary responsibility for the maintenance of international peace and security. Even if otherwise the Security Council (and its permanent members) was willing to refer a situation to the ICC, the newly added jurisdiction for aggression might serve as a further disincentive to do so.

430   Thus, all in all, there is a serious number of challenges faced not only for the ability for the Court to generally be able to exercise its jurisdiction over the crime of aggression, but to the universality of the amendments. So far, the Rome Statute is still short of support from approximately one-third of the world's States. Additionally, there have been threats and actual steps taken by a number of States to actually withdraw their instruments of ratification of aggression to the Rome Statute. In 2016, The Gambia, South Africa and Burundi informed the UN that they were withdrawing from the ICC, while the Philippines did so in 2018. Russia, which had never ratified the Rome Statute, withdrew its signature.

---

[422] Zimmermann, 16 *JICJ* 2018, 19 (27 *et seq.*).

On 31 January 2017, the African Union had called (though in a non-binding   **431**
resolution) for the mass withdrawal of member States from the ICC, while welcoming
and fully supporting "the sovereign decisions taken by Burundi, South Africa and The
Gambia as pioneer implementers of the Withdrawal Strategy".[423] However, in February
2017, The Gambia (after a change of government) officially reversed its decision.[424]
South Africa followed one month later (due to a judgment of a domestic court finding
that the approval of the parliament had to be obtained before the instrument of
withdrawal can be deposited, so that the instrument was unconstitutional and inva-
lid).[425] Burundi's withdrawal became effective as of 27 October 2017 while the one by
the Philippines becam effective as of 18 March 2019.

At its 2018 summit, the African Union adopted a more constructive approach and   **432**
announced that it would aim for seeking (through the UN General Assembly) an advisory
opinion from the ICJ on the question of immunity of high government officials, as well as
interpretative declarations from the ASP on two immunity-related provisions of the Rome
Statute. At the same time, it upheld its resistance against Omar Al-Bashir's arrest warrant
and the ICC's decision to open an investigation in the situation of Burundi as it was held
prejudicial to the peace process under the auspices of the East African Community.[426]
Time will show whether the ICC will indeed have to face a mass exodus of African States,
which, beyond doubt, would constitute a massive threat to its work.

In March 2018, the Philippines, as the first Asian country, notified the UN of its   **433**
withdrawal which took effect in March 2019.[427] This decision has to be considered a
reaction to the ICC's preliminary examinations[428] (starting one month before the withdrawal) into alleged crimes against humanity in the course of the Duterte government's
deadly "war on drugs" campaign. However, it should be noted that, just as it is the case in
the situation of Burundi, the ICC retains its jurisdiction over crimes committed during the
time in which a State was party to the Statute and may exercise this jurisdiction over these
crimes even after the withdrawal becomes effective.[429] With Malaysia, the ICC faced a
considerable U-turn. Having submitted its instrument of accession to the Rome Statute on
4 March 2019, this in accordance with Art. 126 (2) means that Malaysia would have
formally become a State Party on 1 June 2019. On 5 April 2019, the Malaysian Prime
Minister announced the government's decision to "rescind its membership of the Statute"
after domestic criticism of the ratification, including from the Malaysian Royal Family.

Furthermore, the Court still faces significant challenges in its ability to investigate and   **434**
prosecute, even with situations referred to by the UN Security Council. For example, the
Court has failed to move forward since the arrest warrant was issued against Omar Al-
Bashir, the (until April 2019) President of Sudan, for crimes committed in Darfur. He
has travelled to countries that are States parties to the Rome Statute during that time,
without any serious risk of extradition, despite legally binding decisions of the ICC.
However, it is also worth noting that in this regard the ICC seems to attempt to avoid a
future collision course with its contracting parties. In a recent decision of one of its Pre-
Trial Chambers, the ICC found that, absent a Security Council referral "the Court may

---

[423] African Union Doc. EX.CL/1006(XXX), 31 January 2017.

[424] C.N.62.2017.TREATIES-XVIII.10, 16 February 2017.

[425] C.N.121.2017.TREATIES-XVIII.10, 7 March 2017.

[426] African Union Doc. EX.CL/1068(XXXII), 28–29 January 2018.

[427] C.N.138.2018.TREATIES-XVIII.10, 17 March 2018.

[428] Statement of the Prosecutor of the International Criminal Court, 8 February 2018, https://www.icc-
cpi.int/Pages/item.aspx?name=180208-otp-stat. (last accessed May 2019)

[429] ICC, No. ICC-01/17-X-9-US-Exp, Decision Pursuant to Article 15 of the Rome Statute on the
Authorization of an Investigation into the Situation in the Republic of Burundi, Pre-Trial Chamber III,
25 October 2017, mn. 24; Press Release ICC-CPI-20180320-PR1371, 20 March 2018.

not, in principle, […] request a State Party to arrest and surrender the Head of State of a State not party to the Statute."[430] Yet the recent Appeal Chamer judgment of 6 May 2019[431] has reversed that position.

435   Additionally, a significant number of preliminary examinations and investigations are looking at very sensitive situations including the possibility of investigations and prosecutions against UN Security Council members. The UN Security Council's permanent five members also constitute the States that have been traditionally alleged to have either committed acts of aggression against other States, or supporting such acts of aggression by their allies against other States. The sensibility of respective investigations has already been proven: Just one day after the release of an ICC report classifying the Russian annexation of Crimea as an occupation in November 2016, Russia withdrew its signature of the Rome Statute.[432]

436   Yet, for many States, the ICC remains a means to protect their sovereignty, territorial integrity and political independence from such an act, as aggression continues to be a real and legitimate concern. As the UN system has proven to be ineffective at times in preventing and punishing such acts, the ICC would thus be a significant step forward in providing an extra layer of protection for States. Nevertheless, this does not necessarily mean success. Considering the challenges that the Court has already faced in carrying out arrest warrants particularly against higher-level officials, including Heads of States, it would be difficult to see how carrying out such warrants against officials accused of aggression would not come with the same – or even worse – challenges. Enforcement will not be easy and the UN Security Council may not be able to provide any means of executing arrest warrants, for example.

437   Once the necessary threshold of State accession to the amendments was reached, the ASP has seized the opportunity to activate the Court's jurisdiction on the crime of aggression. This gives States that have traditionally not been aggressors, and prone to aggression, interest in supporting and strengthening the Court's jurisdiction over the crime. It also works towards removing the political connotations associated with aggression and towards one that can be dealt with within a judicial institution. While the crime of aggression, as included within the Rome Statute, is the result of the collective of text from the UN Charter, the UN General Assembly's *Friendly Relation Declaration*, and the Assembly's Resolution 3314, its invocations will continue to face serious challenges. While there has been some historical jurisprudence on the crime of aggression as a crime against peace, the jurisprudence is far and few between – largely theoretical and academic. Yet given its status under international law, the prohibition as a peremptory norm that cannot be derogated from, it is only more important to ensure the ICC as a means of preventing it.

438   It remains to be seen how the supporters of the Kampala amendments will move forward on this. On 14 December 2017, the ASP decided to activate the Court's jurisdiction. However, universal support for the amendment will take time. Since 17 July 2018, the Court has been able to exercise its jurisdiction, but with a very limited jurisdiction *ratione personae* as only 38 States have so far ratified the amendment. Just as it had been the case with the Rome Statute in and of itself, also the crime of aggression requires a serious amount of work and resources to move towards reaching universality.

---

[430] *ICC, The Prosecutor v. Omar Hassan Ahmad Al-Bashir*, No. ICC-02/05-01/09, Decision under Article 87(7) of the Rome Statute on the non-compliance by South Africa with the request by the Court for the arrest and surrender of Omar Al-Bashir, Pre-Trial Chamber II, 6 July 2017, mn. 82.

[431] *ICC, The Prosecutor v. Omar Hassan Ahmad Al-Bashir*, No. ICC-02/05-01/09-397, Judgment in the Jordan Referral re Al-Bashir Appeal, Appeals Chamerb, 6 May 2019, mn. 114.

[432] https://www.theguardian.com/world/2016/nov/16/russia-withdraws-signature-from-international-criminal-court-statute (last accessed May 2019).

APPENDIX

1. Rome Statute of the International Criminal Court (excerpts)

Article 5
Crimes within the jurisdiction of the Court

The jurisdiction of the Court shall be limited to the most serious crimes of concern to the international community as a whole. The Court has jurisdiction in accordance with this Statute with respect to the following crimes:

(a) The crime of genocide;
(b) Crimes against humanity;
(c) War crimes;
(d) The crime of aggression.

Article 8 *bis*
Crime of aggression

1. For the purpose of this Statute, "crime of aggression" means the planning, preparation, initiation or execution, by a person in a position effectively to exercise control over or to direct the political or military action of a State, of an act of aggression which, by its character, gravity and scale, constitutes a manifest violation of the Charter of the United Nations.

2. For the purpose of paragraph 1, "act of aggression" means the use of armed force by a State against the sovereignty, territorial integrity or political independence of another State, or in any other manner inconsistent with the Charter of the United Nations. Any of the following acts, regardless of a declaration of war, shall, in accordance with United Nations General Assembly resolution 3314 (XXIX) of 14 December 1974, qualify as an act of aggression:

(a) The invasion or attack by the armed forces of a State of the territory of another State, or any military occupation, however temporary, resulting from such invasion or attack, or any annexation by the use of force of the territory of another State or part thereof;

(b) Bombardment by the armed forces of a State against the territory of another State or the use of any weapons by a State against the territory of another State;

(c) The blockade of the ports or coasts of a State by the armed forces of another State;

(d) An attack by the armed forces of a State on the land, sea or air forces, or marine and air fleets of another State;

(e) The use of armed forces of one State which are within the territory of another State with the agreement of the receiving State, in contravention of the conditions provided for in the agreement or any extension of their presence in such territory beyond the termination of the agreement;

(f) The action of a State in allowing its territory, which it has placed at the disposal of another State, to be used by that other State for perpetrating an act of aggression against a third State;

(g) The sending by or on behalf of a State of armed bands, groups, irregulars or mercenaries, which carry out acts of armed force against another State of such gravity as to amount to the acts listed above, or its substantial involvement therein.

Article 15 *bis*
Exercise of jurisdiction over the crime of aggression (State referral, *proprio motu*)

1. The Court may exercise jurisdiction over the crime of aggression in accordance with article 13, paragraphs (a) and (c), subject to the provisions of this article.
2. The Court may exercise jurisdiction only with respect to crimes of aggression committed one year after the ratification or acceptance of the amendments by thirty States Parties.
3. The Court shall exercise jurisdiction over the crime of aggression in accordance with this article, subject to a decision to be taken after 1 January 2017 by the same majority of States Parties as is required for the adoption of an amendment to the Statute.
4. The Court may, in accordance with article 12, exercise jurisdiction over a crime of aggression, arising from an act of aggression committed by a State Party, unless that State Party has previously declared that it does not accept such jurisdiction by lodging a declaration with the Registrar. The withdrawal of such a declaration may be effected at any time and shall be considered by the State Party within three years.
5. In respect of a State that is not a party to this Statute, the Court shall not exercise its jurisdiction over the crime of aggression when committed by that State's nationals or on its territory.
6. Where the Prosecutor concludes that there is a reasonable basis to proceed with an investigation in respect of a crime of aggression, he or she shall first ascertain whether the Security Council has made a determination of an act of aggression committed by the State concerned. The Prosecutor shall notify the Secretary-General of the United Nations of the situation before the Court, including any relevant information and documents.
7. Where the Security Council has made such a determination, the Prosecutor may proceed with the investigation in respect of a crime of aggression.
8. Where no such determination is made within six months after the date of notification, the Prosecutor may proceed with the investigation in respect of a crime of aggression, provided that the Pre-Trial Division has authorized the commencement of the investigation in respect of a crime of aggression in accordance with the procedure contained in article 15, and the Security Council has not decided otherwise in accordance with article 16.
9. A determination of an act of aggression by an organ outside the Court shall be without prejudice to the Court's own findings under this Statute.
10. This article is without prejudice to the provisions relating to the exercise of jurisdiction with respect to other crimes referred to in article 5.

Article 15 *ter*
Exercise of jurisdiction over the crime of aggression (Security Council referral)

1. The Court may exercise jurisdiction over the crime of aggression in accordance with article 13, paragraph (b), subject to the provisions of this article.
2. The Court may exercise jurisdiction only with respect to crimes of aggression committed one year after the ratification or acceptance of the amendments by thirty States Parties.

3. The Court shall exercise jurisdiction over the crime of aggression in accordance with this article, subject to a decision to be taken after 1 January 2017 by the same majority of States Parties as is required for the adoption of an amendment to the Statute.
4. A determination of an act of aggression by an organ outside the Court shall be without prejudice to the Court's own findings under this Statute.
5. This article is without prejudice to the provisions relating to the exercise of jurisdiction with respect to other crimes referred to in article 5.

2. Resolutions and understandings adopted in Kampala

Resolution RC/Res.6

Adopted at the 13th plenary meeting, on 11 June 2010, by consensus

RC/Res.6
The crime of aggression

The Review Conference,

Recalling paragraph 1 of article 12 of the Rome Statute,

Recalling paragraph 2 of article 5 of the Rome Statute,

Recalling also paragraph 7 of resolution F, adopted by the United Nations Diplomatic Conference of Plenipotentiaries on the Establishment of an International Criminal Court on 17 July 1998,

Recalling further resolution ICC-ASP/1/Res.1 on the continuity of work in respect of the crime of aggression, and *expressing its appreciation* to the Special Working Group on the Crime of Aggression for having elaborated proposals on a provision on the crime of aggression,

Taking note of resolution ICC-ASP/8/Res.6, by which the Assembly of States Parties forwarded proposals on a provision on the crime of aggression to the Review Conference for its consideration,

Resolved to activate the Court's jurisdiction over the crime of aggression as early as possible,

1. Decides to adopt, in accordance with article 5, paragraph 2, of the Rome Statute of the International Criminal Court (hereinafter: "the Statute") the amendments to the Statute contained in annex I of the present resolution, which are subject to ratification or acceptance and shall enter into force in accordance with article 121, paragraph 5; and notes that any State Party may lodge a declaration referred to in article 15 *bis* prior to ratification or acceptance;

2. *Also decides* to adopt the amendments to the Elements of Crimes contained in annex II of the present resolution;

3. *Also decides* to adopt the understandings regarding the interpretation of the above-mentioned amendments contained in annex III of the present resolution;

4. *Further decides* to review the amendments on the crime of aggression seven years after the beginning of the Court's exercise of jurisdiction;

5. *Calls upon* all States Parties to ratify or accept the amendments contained in annex I.

Annex I
Amendments to the Rome Statute of the International Criminal Court
on the crime of aggression

1. *Article 5, paragraph 2, of the Statute is deleted.*

2. *The following text is inserted after article 8 of the Statute:*

Article 8 *bis*
Crime of aggression

1. For the purpose of this Statute, "crime of aggression" means the planning, preparation, initiation or execution, by a person in a position effectively to exercise control over or to direct the political or military action of a State, of an act of aggression which, by its character, gravity and scale, constitutes a manifest violation of the Charter of the United Nations.

2. For the purpose of paragraph 1, "act of aggression" means the use of armed force by a State against the sovereignty, territorial integrity or political independence of another State, or in any other manner inconsistent with the Charter of the United Nations. Any of the following acts, regardless of a declaration of war, shall, in accordance with United Nations General Assembly resolution 3314 (XXIX) of 14 December 1974, qualify as an act of aggression:

(a) The invasion or attack by the armed forces of a State of the territory of another State, or any military occupation, however temporary, resulting from such invasion or attack, or any annexation by the use of force of the territory of another State or part thereof;

(b) Bombardment by the armed forces of a State against the territory of another State or the use of any weapons by a State against the territory of another State;

(c) The blockade of the ports or coasts of a State by the armed forces of another State;

(d) An attack by the armed forces of a State on the land, sea or air forces, or marine and air fleets of another State;

(e) The use of armed forces of one State which are within the territory of another State with the agreement of the receiving State, in contravention of the conditions provided for in the agreement or any extension of their presence in such territory beyond the termination of the agreement;

(f) The action of a State in allowing its territory, which it has placed at the disposal of another State, to be used by that other State for perpetrating an act of aggression against a third State;

(g) The sending by or on behalf of a State of armed bands, groups, irregulars or mercenaries, which carry out acts of armed force against another State of such gravity as to amount to the acts listed above, or its substantial involvement therein.

3. *The following text is inserted after article 15 of the Statute:*

Article 15 *bis*
Exercise of jurisdiction over the crime of aggression
(State referral, *proprio motu*)

1. The Court may exercise jurisdiction over the crime of aggression in accordance with article 13, paragraphs (a) and (c), subject to the provisions of this article.

2. The Court may exercise jurisdiction only with respect to crimes of aggression committed one year after the ratification or acceptance of the amendments by thirty States Parties.

3. The Court shall exercise jurisdiction over the crime of aggression in accordance with this article, subject to a decision to be taken after 1 January 2017 by the same majority of States Parties as is required for the adoption of an amendment to the Statute.

4. The Court may, in accordance with article 12, exercise jurisdiction over a crime of aggression, arising from an act of aggression committed by a State Party, unless that State Party has previously declared that it does not accept such jurisdiction by lodging a declaration with the Registrar. The withdrawal of such a declaration may be effected at any time and shall be considered by the State Party within three years.

5. In respect of a State that is not a party to this Statute, the Court shall not exercise its jurisdiction over the crime of aggression when committed by that State's nationals or on its territory.

6. Where the Prosecutor concludes that there is a reasonable basis to proceed with an investigation in respect of a crime of aggression, he or she shall first ascertain whether the Security Council has made a determination of an act of aggression committed by the State concerned. The Prosecutor shall notify the Secretary-General of the United Nations of the situation before the Court, including any relevant information and documents.

7. Where the Security Council has made such a determination, the Prosecutor may proceed with the investigation in respect of a crime of aggression.

8. Where no such determination is made within six months after the date of notification, the Prosecutor may proceed with the investigation in respect of a crime of aggression, provided that the Pre-Trial Division has authorized the commencement of the investigation in respect of a crime of aggression in accordance with the procedure contained in article 15, and the Security Council has not decided otherwise in accordance with article 16.

9. A determination of an act of aggression by an organ outside the Court shall be without prejudice to the Court's own findings under this Statute.

10. This article is without prejudice to the provisions relating to the exercise of jurisdiction with respect to other crimes referred to in article 5.

4. *The following text is inserted after article 15 bis of the Statute:*

Article 15 *ter*
Exercise of jurisdiction over the crime of aggression
(Security Council referral)

1. The Court may exercise jurisdiction over the crime of aggression in accordance with article 13, paragraph (b), subject to the provisions of this article.

2. The Court may exercise jurisdiction only with respect to crimes of aggression committed one year after the ratification or acceptance of the amendments by thirty States Parties.

3. The Court shall exercise jurisdiction over the crime of aggression in accordance with this article, subject to a decision to be taken after 1 January 2017 by the same majority of States Parties as is required for the adoption of an amendment to the Statute.

4. A determination of an act of aggression by an organ outside the Court shall be without prejudice to the Court's own findings under this Statute.

5. This article is without prejudice to the provisions relating to the exercise of jurisdiction with respect to other crimes referred to in article 5.

5. *The following text is inserted after article 25, paragraph 3, of the Statute:*

3 bis. In respect of the crime of aggression, the provisions of this article shall apply only to persons in a position effectively to exercise control over or to direct the political or military action of a State.

6. *The first sentence of article 9, paragraph 1, of the Statute is replaced by the following sentence:*

1. Elements of Crimes shall assist the Court in the interpretation and application of Articles 6, 7, 8 and 8 *bis.*

7. *The chapeau of article 20, paragraph 3, of the Statute is replaced by the following paragraph; the rest of the paragraph remains unchanged:*

3. No person who has been tried by another court for conduct also proscribed under article 6, 7, 8 or 8 *bis* shall be tried by the Court with respect to the same conduct unless the proceedings in the other court:

Annex II
Amendments to the Elements of Crimes
Article 8 *bis*
Crime of aggression

Introduction

1. It is understood that any of the acts referred to in article 8 *bis*, paragraph 2, qualify as an act of aggression.
2. There is no requirement to prove that the perpetrator has made a legal evaluation as to whether the use of armed force was inconsistent with the Charter of the United Nations.
3. The term "manifest" is an objective qualification.
4. There is no requirement to prove that the perpetrator has made a legal evaluation as to the "manifest" nature of the violation of the Charter of the United Nations.

Elements

1. The perpetrator planned, prepared, initiated or executed an act of aggression.
2. The perpetrator was a person[1] in a position effectively to exercise control over or to direct the political or military action of the State which committed the act of aggression.
3. The act of aggression – the use of armed force by a State against the sovereignty, territorial integrity or political independence of another State, or in any other manner inconsistent with the Charter of the United Nations – was committed.
4. The perpetrator was aware of the factual circumstances that established that such a use of armed force was inconsistent with the Charter of the United Nations.
5. The act of aggression, by its character, gravity and scale, constituted a manifest violation of the Charter of the United Nations.
6. The perpetrator was aware of the factual circumstances that established such a manifest violation of the Charter of the United Nations.

Annex III
Understandings regarding the amendments to the Rome Statute of the International Criminal Court on the crime of aggression

Referrals by the Security Council

1. It is understood that the Court may exercise jurisdiction on the basis of a Security Council referral in accordance with article 13, paragraph (b), of the Statute only with respect to crimes of aggression committed after a decision in accordance with article 15 *ter*, paragraph 3, is taken, and one year after the ratification or acceptance of the amendments by thirty States Parties, whichever is later.

---

[1] With respect to an act of aggression, more than one person may be in a position that meets these criteria.

2. It is understood that the Court shall exercise jurisdiction over the crime of aggression on the basis of a Security Council referral in accordance with article 13, paragraph (b), of the Statute irrespective of whether the State concerned has accepted the Court's jurisdiction in this regard.

Jurisdiction *ratione temporis*

3. It is understood that in case of article 13, paragraph (a) or (c), the Court may exercise its jurisdiction only with respect to crimes of aggression committed after a decision in accordance with article 15 *bis*, paragraph 3, is taken, and one year after the ratification or acceptance of the amendments by thirty States Parties, whichever is later.

Domestic jurisdiction over the crime of aggression

4. It is understood that the amendments that address the definition of the act of aggression and the crime of aggression do so for the purpose of this Statute only. The amendments shall, in accordance with article 10 of the Rome Statute, not be interpreted as limiting or prejudicing in any way existing or developing rules of international law for purposes other than this Statute.

5. It is understood that the amendments shall not be interpreted as creating the right or obligation to exercise domestic jurisdiction with respect to an act of aggression committed by another State.

Other understandings

6. It is understood that aggression is the most serious and dangerous form of the illegal use of force; and that a determination whether an act of aggression has been committed requires consideration of all the circumstances of each particular case, including the gravity of the acts concerned and their consequences, in accordance with the Charter of the United Nations.

7. It is understood that in establishing whether an act of aggression constitutes a manifest violation of the Charter of the United Nations, the three components of character, gravity and scale must be sufficient to justify a "manifest" determination. No one component can be significant enough to satisfy the manifest standard by itself.

3. Resolution ICC-ASP/16/Res.5 adopted on 14 December 2017

Adopted at the 13th plenary meeting, on 14 December 2017, by consensus

ICC-ASP/16/Res.5
Activation of the jurisdiction of the Court over the crime of aggression

The Assembly of States Parties,

Recognizing the historic significance of the consensual decision at the Kampala Review Conference to adopt the amendments to the Rome Statute on the crime of aggression, and in this regard *recalling* resolution RC/Res.6,

Reaffirming the purposes and principles of the Charter of the United Nations,

Recalling its resolve to activate the Court's jurisdiction over the crime of aggression as early as possible, subject to a decision according to paragraphs 3 of article 15 *bis* and article 15 *ter*,

Noting with appreciation the Report on the facilitation on the activation of the jurisdiction of the International Criminal Court over the crime of aggression,[1] which summarizes the views of States Parties,

Recalling paragraph 4 of article 15 *bis* and paragraph 5 of article 121,

Recalling also that in paragraph 1 of RC/Res.6 the Review Conference decided to adopt, in accordance with paragraph 2 of article 5 the amendments regarding the crime of aggression, which are subject to ratification or acceptance and shall enter into force in accordance with paragraph 5 of article 121; and noted that any State Party may lodge a declaration referred to in article 15 *bis* prior to ratification or acceptance of the amendments,

1. *Decides* to activate the Court's jurisdiction over the crime of aggression as of 17 July 2018;

2. *Confirms* that, in accordance with the Rome Statute, the amendments to the Statute regarding the crime of aggression adopted at the Kampala Review Conference enter into force for those States Parties which have accepted the amendments one year after the deposit of their instruments of ratification or acceptance and that in the case of a State referral or *propio motu* investigation the Court shall not exercise its jurisdiction regarding a crime of aggression when committed by a national or on the territory of a State Party that has not ratified or accepted these amendments;

3. *Reaffirms* paragraph 1 of article 40 and paragraph 1 of article 119 of the Rome Statute in relation to the judicial independence of the judges of the Court;

4. *Renews* its call upon all States Parties which have not yet done so to ratify or accept the amendments to the Rome Statute on the crime of aggression.

---

[1] ICC-ASP/16/24.

4. UN General Assembly Resolution 3314 (XXIX) of 14 December 1974 on the *Definition of Aggression*

The General Assembly,

Having considered the report of the Special Committee on the Question of Defining Aggression, established pursuant to its resolution 2330(XXII) of 18 December 1967, covering the work of its seventh session held from 11 March to 12 April 1974, including the draft Definition of Aggression adopted by the Special Committee by consensus and recommended for adoption by the General Assembly,[1]

Deeply convinced that the adoption of the Definition of Aggression would contribute to the strengthening of international peace and security,

1. *Approves* the Definition of Aggression, the text of which is annexed to the present resolution;

2. *Expresses its appreciation* to the Special Committee on the Question of Defining Aggression for its work which resulted in the elaboration of the Definition of Aggression;

3. *Calls upon* all States to refrain from all acts of aggression and other uses of force contrary to the Charter of the United Nations and the Declaration on Principles of International Law concerning Friendly Relations and Cooperation among States in accordance with the Charter of the United Nations;[2]

4. *Calls the attention* of the Security Council to the Definition of Aggression, as set out below, and recommends that it should, as appropriate, take account of that Definition as guidance in determination, in accordance with the Charter, the existence of an act of aggression.

2319th plenary meeting
14 December 1974

ANNEX
Definition of Aggression

The General Assembly,

Basing itself on the fact that one of the fundamental purposes of the United Nations is to maintain international peace and security and to take effective collective measures for the prevention and removal of threats to the peace, and for the suppression of acts of aggression or other breaches of the peace,

Recalling that the Security Council, in accordance with Article 39 of the Charter of the United Nations, shall determine the existence of any threat to the peace, breach of the peace or act of aggression and shall make recommendations, or decide what measures shall be taken in accordance with Articles 41 and 42, to maintain or restore international peace and security,

Recalling also the duty of States under the Charter to settle their international disputes by peaceful means in order not to endanger international peace, security and justice,

Bearing in mind that nothing in this Definition shall be interpreted as in any way affecting the scope of the provisions of the Charter with respect to the functions and powers of the organs of the United Nations,

---

[1] *Official Records of the General Assembly, Twenty-ninth Session, Supplement No. 19* (A/9619 and Corr. 1).
[2] Resolution 2625 (XXV), annex.

Considering also that, since aggression is the most serious and dangerous form of the illegal use of force, being fraught, in the conditions created by the existence of all types of weapons of mass destruction, with the possible threat of a world conflict and all its catastrophic consequences, aggression should be defined at the present stage,

Reaffirming the duty of States not to use armed force to deprive peoples of their right to self-determination, freedom and independence, or to disrupt territorial Integrity,

Reaffirming also that the territory of a State shall not be violated by being the object, even temporarily, of military occupation or of other measures of force taken by another State in contravention of the Charter, and that it shall not be the object of acquisition by another State resulting from such measures or the threat thereof,

Reaffirming also the provisions of the Declaration on Principles of International Law concerning Friendly Relations and Cooperation among States in accordance with the Charter of the United Nations,

Convinced that the adoption of a definition of aggression ought to have the effect of deterring a potential aggressor, would simplify the determination of acts of aggression and the implementation of measures to suppress them and would also facilitate the protection of the rights and lawful interests of, and the rendering of assistance to, the victim,

Believing that, although the question whether an act of aggression has been committed must be considered in the light of all the circumstances of each particular case, it is nevertheless desirable to formulate basic principles as guidance for such determination,

Adopts the following Definition of Aggression:[3]

Article 1

Aggression is the use of armed force by a State against the sovereignty, territorial integrity or political independence of another State, or in any other manner inconsistent with the Charter of the United Nations, as set out in this Definition.

Explanatory note: In this Definition the term "State":

(a) Is used without prejudice to questions of recognition or to whether a State is a member of the United Nations;

(b) Includes the concept of a "group of States" where appropriate.

Article 2

The first use of armed force by a State in contravention of the Charter shall constitute *prima facie* evidence of an act of aggression although the Security Council may, in conformity with the Charter, conclude that a determination that an act of aggression has been committed would not be justified in the light of other relevant circumstances, including the fact that the acts concerned or their consequences are not of sufficient gravity.

Article 3

Any of the following acts, regardless of a declaration of war, shall, subject to and in accordance with the provisions of article 2, qualify as an act of aggression:

(a) The invasion or attack by the armed forces of a State of the territory of another State, or any military occupation, however temporary, resulting from such invasion

---

[3] Explanatory notes on Articles 3 and 5 are to be found in paragraph 20 of the Report of the Special Committee on the Question of Defining Aggression (*Official Records of the General Assembly, Twenty-ninth Session, Supplement No. 19* (A/9619 and Corr. 1). Statements on the Definition are contained in paragraphs 9 and 10 of the report of the Sixth Committee (A/9890).

or attack, or any annexation by the use of force of the territory of another State or part thereof,

(b) Bombardment by the armed forces of a State against the territory of another State or the use of any weapons by a State against the territory of another State;

(c) The blockade of the ports or coasts of a State by the armed forces of another State;

(d) An attack by the armed forces of a State on the land, sea or air forces, or marine and air fleets of another State;

(e) The use of armed forces of one State which are within the territory of another State with the agreement of the receiving State, in contravention of the conditions provided for in the agreement or any extension of their presence in such territory beyond the termination of the agreement;

(f) The action of a State in allowing its territory, which it has placed at the disposal of another State, to be used by that other State for perpetrating an act of aggression against a third State;

(g) The sending by or on behalf of a State of armed bands, groups, irregulars or mercenaries, which carry out acts of armed force against another State of such gravity as to amount to the acts listed above, or its substantial involvement therein.

Article 4

The acts enumerated above are not exhaustive and the Security Council may determine that other acts constitute aggression under the provisions of the Charter.

Article 5

1. No consideration of whatever nature, whether political, economic, military or otherwise, may serve as a justification for aggression.

2. A war of aggression is a crime against international peace. Aggression gives rise to international responsibility.

3. No territorial acquisition or special advantage resulting from aggression is or shall be recognized as lawful.

Article 6

Nothing in this Definition shall be construed as in any way enlarging or diminishing the scope of the Charter, including its provisions concerning cases in which the use of force is lawful.

Article 7

Nothing in this Definition, and in particular article 3, could in any way prejudice the right to self-determination, freedom and independence, as derived from the Charter, of peoples forcibly deprived of that right and referred to in the Declaration on Principles of International Law concerning Friendly Relations and Cooperation among States in accordance with the Charter of the United Nations, particularly peoples under colonial and racist regimes or other forms of alien domination: nor the right of these peoples to struggle to that end and to seek and receive support, in accordance with the principles of the Charter and in conformity with the above-mentioned Declaration.

Article 8

In their interpretation and application the above provisions are interrelated and each provision should be construed in the context of the other provisions.